CANTERBURY

TAILS

This book is dedicated to Mary, my

mother who always told me I should

write a book

Chris Gilberd

Chapter One

Ouch That Smarts

It was a warm sunny Canterbury day in very early spring; the alpacas were sampling the fresh green tendrils of grass as they pushed upwards towards the sunlight.

The view from the upstairs office of our new 'Barn' building was particularly splendid that morning, the Southern Alps seemed very close, their snow covered peaks rising majestically up into the bluest of skies. The foothills and valleys in their various shades of deep blues and purples were visible between the line of huge oak and lime trees that lined the roadway.

It was truly a lovely day to be made "redundant". They would be here soon, the boys from Head Office in Australia to take away the files and computers, the printer, the fax and all my toys, my laptop, my cool cell phone, my corporate credit card, my beautiful company car with its metallic burgundy paintwork, cream leather and wood paneling.

It had been a stressful few months, the New Zealand subsidiary that I had painstakingly brought back from the brink of collapse into substantial profit had not fared well this last year. A major restructuring had seen me for the last three and a half years working from home, more recently in our wonderful purpose built red corrugated steel Barn that also served as guest accommodation and a craft studio/classroom/shop the domain of Elaine, my beautiful and very crafty wife.

Operating the wholesale operation remotely from the comfort of home also meant many days and weeks on the road catching up with retailers, visiting warehouses, organizing advertising campaigns and attending meetings in Aussie and conferences further afield but it had been working well.

That was until a change in senior management. The parent company was Japanese based and the previous two managing directors had been hard task masters but fair and we enjoyed a mutual respect, they rewarded me well in the good times but were also supportive in the tougher periods.

The fact that I had remarried and moved to the country from the city intrigued them and when the subsidiary Head Office started operating from a 15 acre alpaca farm they were quietly delighted and found excuses to bring visiting execs from Tokyo for a look around.

That was until the new smiley guy arrived. Mr Smiley became a bit of an enigma around the company; he appeared to have little understanding of the business and was constantly seeking advice from Tokyo. That was fine for the Australian operation but as New Zealand was a very small part of his turnover he decided he could handle it without assistance.

So began the most frustrating 18 months of my business life, having to stand by as Mr Smiley unraveled all the hard work my team and I had done over the years to build up the business.

Stand by, however was something that I could not do, both as a Director and as a matter of integrity and also due to the responsibility I felt for our retailers who relied on our leading brand for their continued business success.

Suffice to say that it was not long before our business and personal relationship deteriorated, particularly with regard to the cultural differences and at the end of the section by my refusal to bow in matters of honour when by doing so would further damage the company. In other words I explained to him on many occasions, in the nicest possible way, that he was an idiot and needed to listen to me and well, you know the outcome.

It did give me great delight though to know that all the many emails we exchanged that may have been deleted from his computer I left on mine for the new person to read and enjoy and hopefully share with others.

It was a day of many and mixed emotions. A huge weight would be lifted from my shoulders as the huge workload and sense of responsibility for so many people would be cleared. For someone who naturally steered away from confrontations I wouldn't have to go head to head with Mr Smiley anymore and that would have to be a good thing. My days would now be my own; the stress levels could at last recede as I regrouped for the next chapter of my life.

For the last few years Elaine and I had been planning our future and that was to, when the time was right, young children and finances neatly sorted, we could begin our dream of living off the property, Warwickz Farm.

The plan was to increase our modest menagerie of a few sheep and alpacas, chickens and pigeons slowly into a rare breed's farm. While doing our bit for conservation we could at the same time earn an income from the sales of rare animals and fertile eggs, convert our sheep and alpaca into fleeces and yarns and scarves and sweaters.

The Barn would be converted into luxurious but rustic farm stay accommodation and a crafters meeting place and shop.

We would have tours by the coach load of tourists bringing with them their bulging wallets and purses and become a major tourist destination of international repute.

We would become self sufficient with the freezer full of legs of lamb and slabs of steak and chops and pork roasts. The tunnel house would keep us in vegetables all year round and the orchard would supply us with a harvest of sun kissed fruit the surplus of which we would sell at the farmers markets.

The cow would supply us with all the butter cream and cheese we could eat and I was looking forward to one day pouring thick creamy milk over my breakfast cereal before I tucked into my home grown bacon and free range eggs and meadow mushrooms sitting alongside the hothouse tomatoes.

Well that was the plan, the dream, the goal and up to a few months ago we had all the time in the world to ease ourselves comfortably into our new life.

Standing in the race alongside the Barn and having finally handed over my Amex Card and car keys I waved to my fully laden ex colleagues as they slowly drove their way past the paddocks like a funeral cortege, I also waved goodbye to my life as I had known it and turned towards my new life and the cottage and into the comforting arms of Elaine.

We decided that our options were limited, I either found another job which being in my mid forties and living in rural Canterbury would not be easy if I was to get a position anywhere close to what I had had or we brought our 5 year plan ahead 5 years.

Taking a deep breath we decided to take the leap, trust in fate and start living the dream, which sounds all very easy and romantic after a nice bottle of red wine.

Our finances had taken a bit of a beating earlier in the year when the local council had insisted that we put in a state of the art environmentally friendly septic tank for the Barn which we had not budgeted for, as we had intended to run a line to one of the two septic tanks that over -serviced the cottage.

After three months of logically explaining, lobbying and arguing, by Elaine who had taken on the project of resisting this imposition, the Council still maintained that unless we spent the $12,000 and put in the system they would not sign off on the building permit. There unwavering argument was that the ground water level in our area was very high and it was imperative we have one.

You can imagine our mood three months later when while on holiday we received a call from Bruce, a part owner of the property, who was looking after the kids, explaining that we had no water as our artesian well had run dry. So much for the ground water level being very high!

Two weeks later and at 42 metres (28 metres deeper than our previous well) we hit water at some outrageous pressure that turned the hole in the ground into something closely resembling a Texas oil well though not as dark and sticky. The unbudgeted bill of $10,000 was also quite spectacular.

Our finances, never particularly healthy with a young family, were not quite in the red but more on the greyer side of black.

A month or so later I was in the Barn in my new office contemplating the finances and the bills and how dry our 15 acres were, brown and dusty and feeling sorry for the alpacas that would need some hay soon to keep them going.

My eyes drifted across to the neighboring dairy farm that resembled a golf course at a country club so green and lush were the paddocks. The huge irrigator was slowly meandering over the verdant swathe of oasis, one of the several irrigators that had been pumping our well dry.

I could feel a slight burn as grimacing, my eyes returned to our desert like farm and my mind remembered the bills. Dairy farms had been invading the province for years now, taking over arable and sheep farms, removing the shelter belts and converting them into dairy operations. Obviously working in collusion with Satan they were stealing our water and turning their land into paradise and our land into a dry thirsty precursor of hell. Taking another gulp of whisky I realized that they must also be in collusion with the council, those minions of the Devil!

Not being of a religious bent I calmed down and realized that I was though becoming a little too stressed with the situation. I decided that as a man who considered he had a bit of a way with words I should sit down and write a letter to the editor and get it off my chest that way little, knowing how things can so easily get out of hand.

My fairly short but well crafted letter elegantly made my points, apart from a reference to the Council the editor decided he better edit, and was duly published the following day.

It reappeared in the Friday edition of this esteemed broadsheet newspaper as the letter of the week with a headline above it and I was rewarded with a flash Parker pen. My stress levels receded (bear in mind I am still employed at this time), I had got it off my chest and obviously my views were deemed worthy of respect and repetition. I quietly glowed with pride.

I could now move on, or so I thought until I received a phone call from the producer of the country's leading current affairs television programme. He had read my letter while staying with his parents who had similar frustrations to ours on their country property. He asked if I would agree to be part of a show that was covering World Water Day and before we knew it a film crew and a well respected reporter were on the way to Warwickz Farm.

It is amazing how much footage goes into making a television programme compared to what survives to go on screen. My several long speeches to camera and reporter and witty anecdotes and advice to the powers that be and to the country in general were whittled down to about 6 minutes which included about 2 minutes of me actually speaking and didn't feature one of my witticisms.

It was a fun half day though which ended with us racing around the countryside trying to find a large irrigator to film as our dairy farmer neighbor having been tipped off when the producer rang him to see if he wanted to be interviewed (and was declined) had withdrawn his from sight.

Elaine was a little concerned about the effect that my little whisky infused fit of pique that had so snowballed would have on our local, predominantly dairying community.

Fortunately it was not a major problem though I must confess to feeling slightly uncomfortable sitting in the local pub among the mutterings and accusatory looks aimed in my direction.

Chapter Two

Paca Ponderings

Now that I have got all that off my chest I should really begin this collection of stories of life on our farm. How we went from being virtually penniless to Warwickz Farm becoming a popular rare breeds farm stay, with over 40 breeds of creatures from over 20 species and yes, still virtually penniless.

Over the years Elaine and I have been talking about putting the stories of our animals into print and hopefully publishing them one day and as you are now reading this, it looks as if we have been successful.

To protect the innocent and the not so innocent some of the human names in the book have been changed however all the incidents described are based on actual happenings and the stars, all of our wonderful creatures' you will meet along the way and their names are factual.

To give you a little background, Elaine and myself (Chris, sorry about not introducing myself sooner) have been living on Warwickz Farm now with our three boys Dean, Adam and Cody since the early 2000s along with Bruce, the boys father a skeptical old bugger who co-owns the property and is the only one of us with a full time job.

Anyway, here we were on this beautiful sunny day watching our life, symbolized by the procession of vehicles slowly exiting the property, well, um, exit the property.

After a sombre lunch I removed my business clothes and replaced them with my flannel shirt, jeans and gumboots and went off to talk to the alpacas.

Alpacas are great listeners and like great listeners they also listen with their whole faces, watching you and moving their heads in acknowledgment and understanding. Their large soulful eyes are constantly searching yours for enlightenment and wisdom and maybe even some alpaca nuts.

The girls I were talking to were part of our herd of ten and included Holly, an older black girl who had blessed us with young River, a white cria (baby alpaca), a few months earlier. River had taken the opportunity to latch onto his mother's undercarriage while she was standing still and was busy slurping away at her.

My tale of woe that I was sharing with the girls gave way to memories of River and the day he was born. Alpacas are intriguing animals for many reasons that you will discover as you read on, including the way they birth.

On the Alti Plano, the foothills of the Andes of Peru and Chile where alpacas predominantly come from, predators roam around at night and over the centuries alpacas have learnt not to give birth at night for this reason.

As one of the few mammals that do not lick their young clean and dry after birthing they can hang on for up to three weeks until the conditions are right, nice and warm and dry.

It had been a damp early autumn and Holly had been holding on for better weather for over a week and Elaine and I had been on standby for the new arrival. We always like to be handy when cria arrive just in case there are any problems and fortunately over the years there has been very few.

We were two days past shopping day and the groans from the kids as the goodies in the pantry fast depleted were getting louder. The light showers turned into heavier rain, so we decided that we were safe to do a supermarket run.

With a last glance at the nonchalant Holly and a wave to the two well drillers who were delving ever deeper to try to find us some water we were off.

Returning a couple of hours later heavily laden with groceries and the windows steaming up with the hot fish and chips we had just bought for lunch we both glanced towards Holly's paddock.

"What's that?" shouted Elaine as I abruptly pulled up trying to look through the foggy window. What was that indeed, a two headed alpaca with one large anxious black fleecy face at one end and a tiny white bewildered looking one at the other?

As we leaped out of the car into the lightly falling rain thoughts of our tantalizing hot feed of crunchy fish and chips fast receding, our senses were hit by another sensation as a deep rumbling roaring sound began to emanate from the next paddock along.

Looking across we watched the two well drillers leaping for shelter as this geyser of water fired many metres into the air. I stood there watching this surreal spectacle for a second or two until a quick slap on the arm from Elaine brought me back to my senses and we went to join our two headed fleecy beastie.

Holly gave us a most unwelcome look and with a couple more pushes River plopped onto the soft wet grass.

It always fascinates me how fast these little things stand up once they have left their secure lodgings of the last eleven and a half months.

Within 20 minutes this wet, sorry looking little guy was up on his feet and taking his first tentative steps. Once again, nature has taught them that while there may not be any predators around quite yet, they better get their skates on because it will be dark before they know it and you have to learn to walk before you can run.

Elaine went to get a towel for me to dry him off with and a little coat for him to wear while it was wet while I contemplated how clever she was.

Alpacas are camelids, part of the camel family as are llamas and as such, like camels; they have a tendency to spit at each other and on the odd occasion any brave human who decides to mess with their young, particularly new born.

Furthermore, alpacas are ruminants, those animals that have two or three stomachs and so have a choice over what ammunition to fire at any foolhardy two- legger. For major conflict i.e. new born defensive strategies they tend to use their third stomach, the lower one, the one where the once green lush feed has been fermenting for several days in potent digestive juices.

"Here you go" Elaine said as she passed me the towel and cute quilted waterproof coat.

I idly thought for a moment about how less than 5 minutes ago I was looking forward to tucking into a steaming feed of mouth watering fish and chips until Elaine nudged me and told me to hurry up as it was getting cold, as were my chips.

Bravely going where no wise man has gone before I quietly walked up to Holly telling her what a clever girl she was and how hungry I was and, well that was all I got out before the first salvo arrived.

Four of my five senses were assailed by this marvel of nature. First my ears heard the screechy spitting noise, and then my eyes momentarily saw the rapidly approaching light green mist of warmth before my face felt its arrival and my nose, well my poor nose attempted to retract into my head as the overpowering paca

21

perfume settled around it and this was all before I had even got to touch the cria.

Like a combat soldier going over the top I buried my head into my shoulders and took two quick paces towards the enemy and gently but determinedly lifted the little thing into my arms and hot footed it out of range as the tenth spit bomb exploded towards me.

Now at a relatively safe distance Elaine quickly and carefully pulled the coat around its middle and pushed the Velcro strips together and then I quickly checked its nether regions to determine that he was indeed a boy.

I then placed him back on his feet as Holly rapidly approached, her head tilted back, her throat making those telltale sounds of imminent stench, her ears down, as we held our ground knowing, that young River while not her target was her destination and first priority and as long as they continued walking towards each other we were safe from more green wet kisses.

As I say, alpacas are not known as great spitters at humans outside of scenarios such as this one, however unlucky people have got caught in the cross fire involving two or three alpacas having an animated discussion. I have a great tip for people who find themselves in imminent danger of the green kiss and that is to look at the alpacas ears.

I have no idea about the physiology involved but alpacas whose ears are up appear to be unable to spit at you. The danger sign is when the ears go down, as if a valve is being opened and the green torpedo bays are now accessible. So if you feel a little uneasy, have a look at the closest alpaca and if his ears are down and he is making noises and you are within a metre of it then my advice would be to urgently step back and cover your nose.

So there I was with my rumblingly hungry tummy, soaked to the skin and covered in sticky smelly green yuckiness and afterbirth but I had a silly grin on my face as did Elaine who was also wet but not sticky or smelly.

We had added a gorgeous white baby alpaca to our herd and he looked perfect. So perfect was he that he is today a ribbon winning stud alpaca who has graced us and other alpaca owners with many beautiful offspring.

We were still smiling widely as we sat down, freshly showered to our soggy fish and chips.

Chapter Three

Rare Rabbit Rescue

Alpacas are a rare breed but when we first got them and the aracauna chickens before them which are also a rare breed, they are the ones that lay slightly green or blue tinged eggs, we had no idea that one day Warwickz Farm would be a rare breed's farm of some note.

It was only after we became involved with the intriguing Enderby Island rabbit that we decided to do our bit for animal conservation. It was to the Enderby Island hutches that I headed off to on my first day of, well unemployment is such an ugly word, my first day of freedom.

The rustic homemade two storey hutches we had secured a few weeks earlier from a rabbit breeder were warm and cosy and functional but desperately needed a lick of paint and promised to keep me honestly employed for a couple of hours.

25

It would be a useful way to fill in time as I waited for the phone and email to start alerting me to the enthusiastic response of those people I had offered my services to, to keep a few dollars rolling in. Those brilliant presentations I had made to business contacts offering my freelance services as an advertising copywriter and website content provider and business consultant should start to pay dividends very soon I told myself.

Meantime, I dipped my brush into the reddish brown paint and daubed away at the hutch smiling at Xavier our very first Enderby who was sitting in a temporary cage next to me.

Elaine stepped off the verandah and walked towards me, a couple of coffee mugs in her hands, looking at my handiwork.

Passing me my old office mug of steaming coffee she asked "You did clean that out first before you started painting, didn't you?"

"Arr, yeah" I hesitatingly replied.

Frowning slightly she asked "Are you sure?"

"Arr, yeah," I repeated, "with, arr, my hand" I said.

"Right," she replied, "get a scrubbing brush and some water, no" she corrected, "get a brush and some hot water and detergent, its no good painting it when its dirty and it needs to be germ free for Xavier." She said with a loud sigh shaking her head.

Elaine is a retired senior nurse and as well as having a nurse's attitude to hygiene she is also a perfectionist. Well not so much a perfectionist more someone who likes to do things properly or not at all. Contemplating this thought as I cleaned my barely used paint brush I decided it was a very good trait if not one the average male naturally embraces in all its glory.

Xavier watched me intently with his dark brown eyes, dodging the occasional splash as I scrubbed away. He was a beautiful looking rabbit with his wild-like streamlined body of dark grey fur sprinkled with white specks at the tips. It would be such a shame if this breed was soon to be lost forever, I thought.

I imagined how difficult life must have been for the original Enderby Island rabbits. Enderby is the northern most of the

Auckland Island group probably the closest islands before you hit the South Pole and was in error, located on the shipping charts a fair distance south of where it actually was, resulting in the latter half of the 19th Century seeing a number of sailing ships founder on the island.

When the bedraggled and hungry sailors were rescued you can imagine how they insisted that some source of decent food was placed on the island in case they ever had the misfortune to be stranded there again.

Their concerns were listened to and the Victorian Acclimatization Society in Australia arranged with the Melbourne Zoo for some rabbits to be delivered to the docks for transportation to Enderby Island.

You can imagine how these poor rabbits felt, being taken from their fully serviced apartments in nice warm Melbourne and unceremoniously dumped on a sub Antarctic island.

Being an officially uninhabited island in those days no one really knows what actually happened but logically, most of the new arrivals would not have survived their first winter.

Those that did survive were obviously the strongest and due to the adverse conditions Mother Nature decided to take pity on them and within only a few decades they had evolved into a totally different rabbit from the original ones from Melbourne and were officially designated as a new breed to be known as the Enderby Island rabbit.

I looked at Xavier in wonder giving him a grin, stating "Wow, you're a pretty special fur ball buddy, evolving that fast" and went to stroke his head through the cage, fast pulling my hand away as he tried to nip my finger before scampering to the back of the cage.

So why, you may wonder do we have Enderbys in captivity when they should be running free and wild as nature intended?

Well that is because by 1992 the Department of Conservation was becoming increasingly concerned about how the introduced animals, especially the rabbits were undermining and destroying the very rare flora on the island. Some of the plants were unique to Enderby Island and as the rabbits were an introduced species it was decided that they would have to go before the flora did.

The Rare Breeds Conservation Society of Canterbury approached the Dept and they agreed to the capture of some of the rabbits before the cull started. Forty nine rabbits were liberated and found a new sanctuary at Willowbank Wildlife Park in Christchurch, before being released to rare breeders like ourselves to help conserve this precious breed with such an amazing story of evolution.

It would be nice if the story ended here and they all lived happily ever after however that is currently not the case. From the 49 that came off Enderby there are now only one or two hundred. To put that into perspective, if you were to take two wild rabbits and in their ideal world they mated as often as they could and all their young survived and did the same and so on, within 2 years those original two rabbits would be responsible for 1.3 million rabbits.

You can see why New Zealand had a real problem in the early years with rabbit populations.

With Enderby Island being only approximately 700 hectares in size Mother Nature had taught Enderbys how to curb their breeding instincts so as not to overpopulate the Island and face starvation.

Unfortunately these instincts still apply and they are very hard to breed. We also have a suspicion the conditions in New Zealand are probably too kind for them as far as climate is concerned and they are probably too well cared for. There is always a risk when mankind interferes, no matter how good his intention, with the ways of nature.

Glancing at my handiwork I was pleasantly surprised to see that during my musings I had painlessly accomplished my task. The tired old weather beaten double hutch unit while still thirsty for paint was at least now very clean, but too wet to paint for a while.

I stretched my legs and surveyed the other Enderbys watching me, their hutches shaded from the hot afternoon sun by the row of tall pine trees they backed on to.

Approaching Beethoven's hutch it suddenly dawned on me that I was probably looking at the world's rarest rabbit. While Enderbys are certainly very rare, Beethoven was even more precious.

Gently, but very firmly I lifted him up and into my arms making sure his back and bottom was supported and his legs unable to find any purchase to spring out of my arms from. Being essentially still a wild rabbit we had trained ourselves to handle them much more securely than with our domestic ones.

Beethoven was a crème Enderby, a very light fawn apricot colour with black points on his nose and ears. Crème Enderbys have been found, through researching the original rabbits from Melbourne Zoo, to be a genetic throwback going back to the original bloodlines emanating from the United Kingdom.

Beethoven was one of only a dozen or so Crème Enderbys in existence and was very special. Little did I know then that Beethoven was also to almost become the worlds rarest road kill twelve months later?

It was a stinking hot February day the following year and I was wearing a singlet and some rugby shorts when I decided it would be good to do a piece on Beethoven to go in the Warwickz Farm Newsletter that was sent out to friends, visitors and guests and whoever wanted a copy, full of updates of life and animals on the farm.

I needed some photos to go with it and had climbed over the wire netting perimeter of the Enderby enclosure where the bunnies were free to hop about and let Beethoven out to hopefully create some great photo opportunities for me.

Having taken quite a few I then, as you do, reviewed them on my digital camera, nice, nice one, delete, delete, really nice one, delete, delete, delete. Crouching down to take some more I noticed a lot of empty space where Beethoven had so recently been and held my breath as I did a quick scan trying to locate him.

There he was, on the wrong side of the netting idling gnawing on a twig. With my pulse starting to quicken I considered my options. Bearing in mind he is basically a wild animal and further, a prey animal whose first instinct is to flee, my options were few.

Stealthily climbing over the netting I prepared to slowly take one of the two large paces he was away from me but as I did so he hopped two more paces away from me now doubling the distance.

I was very aware of the noise of the vehicles racing down the highway on the other side of the trees particularly as that was the direction Beethoven was headed.

I tentatively took another step forward wincing as Beethoven reciprocated with another long couple of hops. He was now closer to the highway than he was to me.

As major concern morphed into rising panic I quietly retraced my steps in order to halt Beethoven's remorseful hops in the direction of imminent violent death. Stepping behind a hedge bordering part of the garden I sprinted across to the next opening in the hedge which brought me out on the other side of Beethoven so that he was between me and the enclosure both of us now parallel to the highway to hell.

Like a chess master I skillfully and tactically moved my quarry step by step back towards the enclosure and safety until finally he was back through the gap and I thankfully reached down to pick him up.

Nothing important in life is ever easy and so it was that with my fingers tantalizingly inches from him Beethoven leapt into action and hopped into the middle of the stand of pine trees behind the enclosure and through another gap in the netting!

With mounting frustration I dived in after him only to watch his little cotton tail escape into the sheep paddock. All the while I was wondering, in horror when Elaine was going to come over to call me in for lunch and discover what a wonderful rare breed's farmer I really was. She would be hopping too, hopping mad.

Joining Beethoven in the sheep paddock I once again did a wide detour and edging close to him dived again at him missing by a rabbit's leg and realizing that if I was to lose sight of him than he was going to be history and so probably was I.

That was when he burst into life and disappeared from sight into and then on a second burst, through the pine trees.

Sweating profusely, adrenaline finally setting in big time, I threw myself in a swan dive head first into the base of the pine trees and then with a classic rugby tackle back, into the enclosure, where my fingers grasped Beethoven around his midriff in triumph.

I stood up in victory with a huge grin on my face, holding Beethoven tight against myself, listening to the applause of the crowd, or come to think of it maybe that was the roaring in my ears from all the adrenaline.

It was only after I had popped Beethoven back into his hutch and my anxiety levels subsided that the throbbing pain began to arrive. I tentatively patted myself down with several agonizing winces and my hand came away with blood on it and also the tattered remains of my ripped singlet.

It is amazing how those jagged little broken branches at the base of pine trees can do so much damage as a human body hurtles against them at breakneck speed, but than again maybe not so surprising.

Stemming the blood flow slowly oozing out of my thigh and neck gashes I made my way inside for a hot shower and a clean up.

"What have you been up to this morning?" Elaine enquired unseen, from the lounge room, working away at her spinning wheel as she heard me limp down the hallway.

"Oh not much, just doing a bit of work around the Enderby enclosure." I replied, heading for the bathroom.

Chapter Four

Grasping the Dream

The first three months of our new lifestyle were a bit of a rollercoaster of emotions. Not having huge financial reserves there was not a lot in the coffers after we had replaced the car, computer, phone etc especially bearing in mind the unbudgeted cost of the septic tank and artesian well, memories of which that still irked me.

We had for several years, every Friday, been enjoying a lovely lunch at a nearby restaurant. The generous antipasto platter with a superb bottle of Shiraz followed by a shared slab of homemade cheesecake washed down with a cappuccino with cinnamon sprinkled on top was our regular treat and something we really looked forward to.

Reluctant to give up this simple pleasure we decided to continue it but fortnightly not weekly, then later monthly as we waited for my long delayed payout to arrive.

I was taking a sip of Shiraz as I contemplated my next mouthful of perhaps blue cheese and artichoke or sundried tomato and brie when my cell phone sung to me.

It was my employment attorney with some good news and some bad news. The good news was that my out of court settlement payout (yes I had challenged my redundancy) had at last arrived but the bad news was that it was half the agreed amount, which had not been particularly significant in the first place.

Mr. Smiley had invited me to challenge the situation in Court if I wanted to, fully aware that corporate lawyers could spin it out until any gain would be lost in legal fees, a view confirmed by my lawyer who also informed me he would now be sending me his invoice.

So ended our final Friday afternoon treat as we headed home to our new reality. Any mild sense of denial we may have had was gone. Our little buffer, as we eased into a self sufficient lifestyle, had now been slashed and we had work to do.

Our website had been up for a few months now and did look very attractive but there were not many people visiting it. The website guy who had been recommended to us had done a great job designing the framework and I told him I would take care of the content and marketing side of it.

It really did showcase the farm with its gentle attractive contours which were unusual here on the Plains and the animals and gardens and Barn Stay room but it needed to start generating business and quickly.

I began researching website marketing and search engine optimization and learning computer code and it wasn't very long, through a combination of linking with other sites, using key words and meta tags and so on that visitor numbers did start showing an increase. We were delighted to receive an official Google page ranking for our home page of 0/10 which was in fact a breakthrough as prior to that Google did not even know we were there to rank.

It was with great excitement that we received an email through warwickzfarm.com one afternoon enquiring about a week's accommodation in the Barn.

An academic from the renowned Mayo Clinic in the States had been doing some research involving the impact of spending extended period's of time at very high altitudes in aircraft and rather than spending months in the air at huge cost had decided to conduct tests on the staff at the US Antarctic Base where the air pressure was the same as at altitude.

The project completed, she was about to head home but wanted to spend some time adjusting herself back into non polar conditions and generally have some time to just relax in the sunshine somewhere nice and safe for a single woman, somewhere green and friendly where she could thaw out and we apparently fitted her bill.

Yes, our first guest was going to be arriving to stay with us from the South Pole!

We had test run the Barn as bed and breakfast accommodation when my elderly parents had visited from Australia late the year before and everything appeared fine: A nice cosy bed, a warm room, TV, DVD player and stereo that all worked, a toilet that flushed and a shower that was user friendly.

It was thus with confidence but with a little trepidation as first time hosts that we confirmed her dates and looked forward to her arrival.

She replied that she was delighted she was coming and could we pick her up from Christchurch. Yes we quickly replied, not a problem.

Elaine and I looked at each other with beaming faces; we were at last in the hospitality business and not unemployed.

How easy it was all going to be. People would go to the website, make a booking, come and sleep in the room, have a breakfast and give us money, next please ching ching.

Coming inside from feeding the chooks an hour or so later I said to Elaine a slight frown on my face, "This Debbie woman coming from the South Pole, she needs picking up right?" I asked.

"Yes, you know that." Elaine replied.

"Okay, work with me here, she doesn't have a car and we live in the country, what is she going to do for her meals, apart from breakfast for 6 days?" I asked.

"Well, we will have to feed her I suppose." Elaine said a frown now starting to crease her face too.

"Hmmm" I responded.

Elaine's frown turning into a big grin as she said to me,

"It's a good thing you've got me isn't it, I've already sent her an email explaining this and she's happy to pay an extra $180.00 for her meals."

"Ching ching " I said reaching out to give her a hug.

43

My beautiful wife was raised in the country unlike myself and spent her earlier years growing up on a chicken farm. It is no longer a chicken farm but apart from the railway carriages Elaine used to play in as a child the place is still pretty much as it was then. Rambling orchards and free range chooks and cats and big old trees surround the ancient old white settler's cottage with its welcoming verandah facing the country lane.

This was obviously the early source of her country wisdom and no nonsense attitude to life, things that were to keep us safe and get us out of trouble over the years here on Warwickz Farm.

Debbie duly arrived and was a delightful introduction into the slightly scary world of being responsible for a stranger's safety and security and well being.

An older lady who was obviously missing her family, Debbie took an instant liking to young Cody whom she spoiled rotten throughout the week. Even a year later she was still

44

corresponding with him and sending him packs of 'yugioh' cards to add to his rapidly expanding collection.

Easy to please and thankfully feed, Debbie enjoyed her time with us relaxing in a green environment for a change and enjoying the alpacas.

Asking whether we offered tours as an optional extra for our guests, having no idea she was in fact our first one, we immediately replied that we did and tentatively offered a price that she happily accepted. A couple of enjoyable days were spent touring the antique shops of the greater Christchurch area and visiting Rakaia Gorge and Arthurs Pass in the heart of the breathtakingly gorgeous Southern Alps.

We said our farewells to Debbie, who had arrived as a guest and left us as a friend, packing her and her numerous cases and lovely craft purchases from the Barn into one very cramped little car.

Waving to her before driving away from the airport I took a great deal of satisfaction knowing that we had enjoyed a good week, made a reasonably large wad of money and probably most of all that Debbie still had no idea that she was our very first guest and one from the South Pole to boot. Not a bad way to start off in the hospitality/tourism business I thought, ching ching.

It turned out to be an extraordinarily good way to kick off but unfortunately it was an aberration. It was to be many years before we would enjoy such stays on a regular basis and even then only during the peak seasons, however we had indeed kicked off and we were officially living off the property.

A few weeks later though the bills were starting to mount up and the income streams were but a trickle and the nights were becoming restless. We were basically living off the last of our savings and the settlement money was fast depleting.

Our planning was good and we could see how it could all work out in the future and we were taking bookings for tours and the odd nights accommodation but the stress levels were rising along with our anxiety and insomnia. We needed an injection of regular cash to tide us over.

We had withdrawn from the consumer society, the cocktail cabinet was dry and we discovered what little treasures could be found in second hand shops. While we may not have looked it we had become members of the survivor society.

Enough is enough I thought, I will just have to get a job, any job to get us back on our feet I decided. By now my soft pink businessmen's hands had hardened up so I would probably be fine on a road gang somewhere I thought soberly.

Scanning the local rag I noticed a jobs vacant advert, one of the few, for a cleaner's position at a nearby University. I decided I would make an appointment and announced my intentions to Elaine.

Lowering her head she slowly nodded to herself then looked up at me a smile radiating from her beautiful face.

"Chris", she said, "If you go to work our whole dream will collapse, we need you to run the farm, I'm too small to deal with the larger animals and anyway I've already had an interview and I start on Monday, 3 hours a night, week nights."

I stood there stunned, utterly stunned.

"I will be free during the day to help with guests and tours and catering and things and...."

Interrupting her I said, "But you're retired, after all those long years this is now your time to relax and...."

Interrupting me this time, Elaine stated in her no nonsense tone "For Gods sake you make me sound like an old woman, we need money and I'm going to get some. I'm sick and tired of not being able to sleep for worrying."

That was my gal and I knew from her tone of voice that the issue was over with. I also knew that now I would really have to step up to the plate as well.

Chapter Five

Sheep Yarns

For quite a few years now Elaine had kept a flock of coloured sheep in the back paddock, mainly Romney's and the odd merino whose fleeces she used for spinning and selling on to other spinners and crafters.

Their colours went from black to white and just about every sheepy tone in between, but predominantly as far as I could tell mainly various shades of brown.

One evening Elaine called me over to her computer and asked me what I thought of the unusual looking sheep she had on her screen.

"What's that funny looking beastie" I asked as I stared at a rangy looking brownie, blackie ram with splotches of white on him and over his neck and spectacular wraparound horns and a smug superior look on his face. "Those horns are pretty cool." I added.

"It's an arapawa ram" she informed me "a native New Zealand feral sheep from Arapawa Island in the Marlbourough Sounds" she added "and I want one, well some actually" she continued.

"No, no," I said, "there are no native animals in New Zealand except birds and marine life" I continued authoritatively. "I think someone's trying to sell you a story.

My authoritative academic air fell away as Elaine having researched the sheep and their history and wool quality over the preceding hours then brought me up to speed on this interesting breed.

Arapawa Island is a relatively large and remote island in Cook Strait the seaway separating New Zealand's North and South Islands. Windswept and wild, it became home to some merino sheep that like the Enderby Island rabbits were dropped off probably by whalers as a source of meat for stranded sailors.

Like the rabbits, due to the harsh conditions on such an exposed Island these feral sheep evolved into their current form in order to survive.

They are highly resistant to foot rot and their fleece will only grow so long before they shed their wool naturally.

Their high resistance to fly-strike had led to research on the breed being conducted to introduce this characteristic into a new "no fuss" sheep breed.

"I think as a rare breed's farm Warwickz Farm should invest in a few of them to do our bit for conservation and give me some more felting options" Elaine stated."

"Arr, I think we may have a current cash flow issue that you may have forgotten about" I replied, my words dripping with sarcasm.

"Not if they're free" Elaine said triumphantly, game set and match to her.

A couple of days later a fellow rare breeder from the West Coast who was trying to downsize his flock bounced his trailer into our driveway with two weird looking ewe lambs and a funny looking ram lamb on board.

Driving into the back paddock to unload them the Coaster watched our faces as the lambs rather than jumping down off the trailer jumped up with a huge bound, once the cover was lifted from the top of the trailer and then continued bouncing across the paddock as if their legs were spring loaded.

"Funny little buggers eh?" their chauffeur said, shaking his head at the offer of a cuppa and heading back down the highway.

We have let these funny little buggers breed with the black and coloured flock over the years and as a result we have a particularly hardy and healthy flock.

The young ram grew into a magnificent creature called Wedge with a real trophy set of merino like horns that grow to about a metre long stretched out.

It was his horns that earned him his name. By the time he had matured he would always give us grief when we were running the sheep through the yards for shearing, drenching and so on.

There would be a hold up in the crush, and inevitably it would always be Wedge whose handlebar horns had got stuck on each set of rails and we would have to climb across and twist them loose to get the traffic moving again.

Always aloof but ready for a good bounce and alert to the goings on in his paddock Wedge was a true patriarch keeping the younger rams under control and making sure all the girls were happily satisfied in the romantic department.

A very good thing about Wedge was that while he was certainly no pet and kept a very healthy distance from humans when at all possible, he never once tried to charge anyone nor have any of his sons.

Wedge passed away last season but his son Wedge the Second is truly his father's son and looks identical to him and has taken over his mantle with ease.

Wedge lives on however, on the pages of a Creative Fibre magazine and also a Black and Coloured Sheep Association publication and his head displaying his resplendent horns is currently sitting on the roof of a shed next to the hay barn much to Elaine s dismay.

A wonderful bonus to having Arapawa sheep that we were not aware of when we got them was the magic that takes place when an Arapawa and a merino get together, some kind of alchemy takes place and in due course these beautiful panda lambs arrive to adorn the nursery paddock.

Very similar to the Jacob sheep from the United Kingdom in appearance we either get white lambs with black spots/markings or black ones with white spots/markings. It is always a delightful highlight of the year when at lambing these cute creatures appear.

We now have two flocks of sheep at either end of the farm, the other one consists of orphan lambs that we have hand fed and over the years and their off spring and later, their offspring. Nova, our first orphan lamb you will meet a little later is now a great grandmother.

We also have a small flock of Gotland Pelt sheep. These intriguing sheep originate from the Island of Gotland, a dependency of Sweden situated in the Baltic Sea. In the 1920s the native sheep of Gotland Island, the Gute where selectively bred with a variety of sheep including ancient Viking ones to create today's hornless, even coated, even bodied Gotland Pelt Sheep.

The pelts are highly prized in Europe in the creation of fashion garments, hence the name Gotland *Pelt*. Closer to home, many of the stunning garments used in the making of The Lord of the Rings trilogy were made from the Gotland Pelts soft curly fleece which is also sought after by spinners and felters.

Warwickz Farm was delighted to be approached by Peter Jacksons production company 3 Foot High (the height of a Hobbit) and we proudly supplied five Gotland Pelt fleeces for use as props in The Hobbit movie along with some rare breed turkey and goose feathers.

Farmed on a small scale only in Sweden as a multi-purpose wool and meat breed there are only approximately 80,000 Gotland Pelts, 1000 of which are now being farmed in New Zealand.

Gotland Pelt Sheep with their black heads and grey bodies are very curious and friendly being closer in personality and appearance to goats than to sheep and it didn't take long once Elaine discovered them that some settled in at Warwickz Farm.

As a fast growing rare breed's farm we decided we had to find a handsome ram for our girls to do our bit for conserving the breed so along came Harry.

Gotland rams have a reputation for jumping over fences which is not good especially when you live by the highway and are surrounded by other farms. That was why before we bought Harry we were assured that he was guaranteed not to be a jumper.

After a couple of days on the farm Harry started to pay a lot of attention to the dozens of ewes across the fence at Mr.

Thompsons sheep farm, in fact after a few days he was busy pacing up and down the fence line talking to the girls next door.

One morning as I was doing the rounds I noticed that Harry was not by the fence and I thought that was good as he must be settling down to life on Warwickz Farm, however on closer inspection I discovered he was gone and looking over the fence far into the distance of Mr. Thompsons farm I saw this grey creature running around with all these beautiful white ewes. So much for not being a jumper I cursed.

Struggling over the barbed wire fence I took off in pursuit trying to divert Harry from the girls he was chasing but after 10 minutes I was doubled over breathless and facing the reality that I would have to find the farmer, politely advise him of the situation and call on his assistance to solve our mutual problem. This I was definitely not looking forward to.

I jogged across three large paddocks to the farmhouse and the farmer's wife giving me a worried look, said Mr. Thompson was in the shearing shed along the road and she would go and tell him, I said I would go back to Harry and wait for him.

After a long walk back to where Harry and his new girlfriends were and a short wait I heard Mr. Thompson bouncing across the paddock with his sheep dog barking on the back of his ute. He skidded to a stop next to me glaring at me with a not so hospitable look on his face and I got in the passenger seat and gave him a sweet smile and apologized about Harry.

We decided we would have to round up the flock and run them down to the yards. Under normal circumstances this would have been quite enjoyable, using the ute and the dog to herd them all together and run them through the gates and finally to the yards. This was much more fun than doing it on a push bike as I was used to on Warwickz Farm.

When we had them in the yards Mr. Thompson who is quite an elderly man, having worked on the farm for over 50 years advised me that he was getting too old to tackle rams and left me to catch Harry.

On the fourth lap around the yards, and much to old Mr.Ts amusement, I leapt on Harry's back and finally managed to grab him. We tied his legs together and I put together a makeshift halter and lead made out of binder twine on him and we put him in the back of the ute. We delivered him back to the fence dividing the properties and we both manhandled him over it and he was now safely back on Warwickz Farm, nearly two hours after I found him gone.

I apologized again to Mr. T but he smiled at me (I think he quite enjoyed the round up) and said in fact Harry had got through the day before and he had not jumped the fence but burrowed under it and it was half Mr. Ts fault for not repairing it properly which he then proceeded to do. I told him we would also attach a car tyre and a lead to Harry so he wouldn't get away again. I once again apologized on both Harry and my behalf after Mr. T explained that he was keeping that particular flock of ewes out of lamb this season and that he would drop any grey little things that arrived in spring over the fence for us.

You would think that that would be the end of this story, however two days later Harry was gone again, a grey blur in the distance on Mr. T's farm. He had somehow wriggled under the fence again taking the tyre with him and I really did not want to bother Mr. Thompson a second time. Fortunately as Harry was slowed down by his tyre bouncing along behind him after about 30 minutes I was able to run him down and managed to drag him back out of sight of Mr.Ts house to the paddock next to our place where we both collapsed in a gasping heap and got our breaths back.

After another 10 minutes of dragging him back to Warwickz Farm I tied him to the fence and waited for Bruce to come home from work and give me a hand getting him back over the fence.

We then found a chain and anchored it to a willow tree and tied

the tyre to the chain and finally he was secure at last.

It turned out that one of Novas grandsons had matured a little

earlier than we had expected and had been happily looking after

our girls before Harry's arrival, hence his interests in the girls

next door.

Not wanting to keep Harry tied to the tree any longer than was

necessary we were fortunately able to, within a few days, recoup

his cost and find him a more secure home where he wouldn't

have to jump or tunnel his way to true love.

Another interesting fact about Gotland Pelt sheep is that like

Arapawa sheep, if they are not shorn when fully fleeced they will

shed their wool. The new fleece will start growing under the old

one and eventually the last season's wool will start to shed as it

catches on tree branches, fences and so on.

It was as Elaine and I were crossing the Gotland paddock that lies between the Barn and the cottage that we came up behind Hermione and noticed that her fleece was coming away at the her neck.

Quietly sneaking up behind her I reached across and grabbed a piece of it in each hand and with a start she leapt forward and I found I was cleanly holding wool from her neck and now her shoulders. Elaine went inside to find some scissors.

While she was gone Hermione took me for a ski around the paddock all the while the fleece that I was gripping tightly was coming away freely and evenly. By the time Elaine got back I was standing there with a silly expression on my face holding the whole blanket in my hands, literally a sheepskin rug but without the skin and a live and happy sheep in the paddock.

The underside was all felted, though with the beginnings of some holes that would have inevitably snagged on things ripping the wool away. The new fleece had been pushing the old fleece away and it had felt like I was pulling against Velcro and as long as I held it evenly it came off in one piece.

It is such an extraordinary story, pulling a fleece off a sheep's back that I am sure many of our visitors think it is a bit of a tall tale and I take great delight in watching their faces as when their tour concludes in the Barn I show them our skinless sheepskin rug.

Discussing the experience with a vastly experienced and renowned rare breeder and animal conservationist he gave the impression that he was absolutely disgusted that some Johnny-come-lately lifestyle blocker could stumble across something that he had been trying to do for many years. It seems that the window of opportunity to do what I did so accidently is very small and depends on several factors including the state of the weather, the sheep and the wool and so on.

Maybe this was an omen that our luck was a-changing.

Chapter Six

Tourism Operators

While we were waiting for the farm stay/bed & breakfast part of the business to crank up we decided to focus on the farm tour side of the operation.

We now had a reasonable menagerie of creatures great and small to make us an unusual and hopefully interesting place to visit and invest a few dollars.

Before the five year plan was so brutally brought forward Elaine had over the years advertised for and successfully received several visits from mainly seniors groups, who came to feed the alpacas, wander through the gardens and have a Devonshire Tea and appeared to thoroughly enjoy themselves.

The gardens had been a good draw card as they transformed from a rambling country garden with curious little pathways and bridges to secret gardens, a fernery and a more formal garden closer to the cottage.

A Farm and Garden Tour page was added with tempting and alluring photos to the website offering tours for $10.00 an adult, $5.00 a child or family passes for $25.00. Then we set about planning for larger tours.

An older couple we had known for years offered to help kick things off as they were part of a "Friendly" social group who occasionally went out on a days outing.

We offered them a lovely tour with a very tasty homemade finger food lunch followed by part two of the tour ending up at the Barn to inspect and enjoy the crafts.

Elaine and I were quite excited about this new income stream however that excitement turned into nervous panic when a few days before the event our friends rang us to confirm the numbers, there would be approximately 30 on the coach!

"Thirty, which is three oh mouths to feed?" I numbly asked Elaine.

"On a coach, where are we supposed to park that" was Elaine's bewildered reply.

Action stations, all available hands on deck, lets see that makes one and ah, two of us I thought, my mind starting to race. Okay 'don't panic Mr. Mainwaring.'

While I started racing around the room not panicking Elaine sat down and started making a list of easy but tasty edibles and their ingredients before going to the computer to calculate the number of serves required for 30 people. Damn, she copes well in a crisis I thought admiringly.

I rushed outside to find a saw to start trimming the macrocarpa hedge line so a coach could hopefully fit up the races without scratching its nice shiny paintwork and hopefully turn around in the paddock behind the Barn. I didn't think the driver would take too kindly to having to back all the way back to the main gate.

Surveying the not insignificant task ahead of me I decided to postpone it temporarily and go back inside.

"Have you got a list of the stuff we need?" I asked Elaine, "I better go into town and get it so we can get things moving." I continued.

"For God sakes, just chill out" she commanded, "remember we promised them a fresh home made lunch, so we will have to make it that morning." She continued. "So there's plenty of time."

"The same morning?" I asked, my eyes widening.

"They are arriving around 10.00am, so if we are up by 6.00am that will give us 4 hours but if you're worried we can get up at 5.00am." Elaine calmly stated.

I stood there quietly and rationally contemplating what she had said before racing out the door as I mumbled something about pruning and coaches.

It was a fast and satisfying learning curve the morning of the tour.

Not able to sleep too well during the night I was up at 5.00am transforming our homely cottage kitchen, built around an ancient coal range, into a spotless and sparkling expanse of smooth hygienically clean surfaces and work areas.

Never having worked with Elaine in this kind of work environment before I was pretty sure that what I had achieved would be her minimum standard required to get the job done right as was confirmed with the glowing smile I received when she joined me at 6.00am.

So began the hours of slicing, dicing, tasting, chopping, mixing, whipping, tasting, spooning, stirring, tasting and spreading.

"Would you please stop putting your fingers in your mouth, now go and wash them again Chris!" she admonished for the sixth time.

After a short break at 7.30am for a coffee as the kids, barely noticing the change in our routine, scoffed a quick breakfast, grabbed their lunches and headed out the door to the school bus, we were back into it.

69

As the hours slipped by a variety of attractive looking and very tasty morsels were created. I was very proud of my contributions which included curried eggs and salmon and avocado crunches.

These were so easy to make and looked and tasted so good. While the French stick that I had sliced into rounds the tops of which I had delicately painted with oil, were under the grill becoming crunchy I mixed a small can of salmon into a bowl of cream cheese until it all dissolved into a creamy texture.

A squeeze of lemon juice was quickly mixed in and it was ready to spread on top of the cooling slices. I then decorated them with fine slivers of gherkin and tomato. The avocado version was decorated with slivers of strawberry and gherkin.

I have always been a great fan of crunchy creamy things and so too have our luncheon guests over the years it seems. It used to concern me a little in the early days as I watched these happy faces opening and closing over these yummies that there would be no leftovers for me, the creator extraordinaire of these delights. Fortunately Elaine noticed my hungry body language and thereafter always used to hold a small selection back for me for when the tourists had taken their swollen bellies home.

Thirty minutes before Showtime we both stood back and admired our handiwork. Every serving space in the kitchen as well as the dining table held platters and servers and plates adorned with sausage rolls, club sandwiches, avocado and salmon crunches, curried eggs, asparagus rolls, fruit kebabs (kiwi fruit, strawberry, pineapple and melon on skewers), caramel crunch slices, fruit cake and scones.

Everything freshly created prepared and garnished and looking divine. Checking the clock we collapsed into a couple of chairs gasping for a cup of tea.

Signaling the coach as it pulled over to the shoulder of the highway I ushered it inside the gates. With a hydraulic whoosh the door opened and I climbed aboard instructing the driver to follow his nose up the race, round the bend and on up to the Barn where he could park while I greeted his passengers.

As I was grabbing for the microphone like a true tour professional the driver touched my wrist and enquired whether the race was wide enough for him to drive through safely. Discreetly crossing my fingers I advised him that it was no problem.

Smiling happily at the sea of older faces smiling back at me and not particularly nervous, as I was used to public speaking, I realized that I had no idea what I was about to say to them.

It went something along the lines of my name is Chris, welcome to Warwickz Farm a rare breeds farm and so on. I remembered that Elaine had told me to make sure I said something to get us out of any potential strife if there were any mishaps so I advised them that we would take all care but no responsibility for them and if they wanted to climb trees and fell out of them then that was their look out which I think covered it pretty well as well as getting a laugh.

I also advised them that Elaine was busy in the kitchen putting together some stale sandwiches and weak tea for them, and got another good laugh. The coach had made the short journey unscathed and there were lots of smiles and the ohhing and ahhing at the alpacas and as we pulled up and I had a good feeling that things were going to work out okay.

Apart from the logistics of suddenly catering for 30 people we also had the problem of finding suitable tables and seating.

The serving area was not a problem as we have a lovely purpose built sheltered barbeque area where we enjoy dining in the warmer months. The outside dining table with an ancient trestle table butted up against it at one end was ideal for a smorgasbord arrangement.

The six outdoor dining area chairs were a start, we just had to come up with another 26 and some tables and we were fine, I thought frowning, my eyes scanning the area for inspiration.

It is amazing how many things you accumulate over the years without realizing it. An old park bench sitting hidden and unused for years in the fernery was tidied up and covered in a gingham table cloth which would accommodate another six skinny bottoms, which left only 20 more to find.

A thankfully large round outdoor plastic table with six chairs plus another four I found in an old shed added to the tally.

Sweating on the last ten I remembered with a smile that our new Barn had a couple of tables and plenty of chairs in and around it and so began a slow furniture shuttle across the paddock.

We were lucky enough a few months later, after a long country drive to a quiet country restaurant to pick up a matching set of four wooden slatted tables and eighteen chairs. They were being updated, some needing minor repairs and we bought them for a song as it seemed, no one was prepared to travel to pick them up. From then on we have really looked the business.

This first tour was a great success. While we did not have the menagerie that we do today we still had plenty of weird and wooly animals they could get up close to and touch.

It seemed that the highlight of the day which was later confirmed by our friends was the luncheon. They told us that quite literally a lot of their visits over the years had indeed culminated in weak tea, soggy sandwiches and stale scones.

As Elaine and I served them teas and coffees I must admit to having mixed feelings as I watched them come back for seconds and thirds as the feast dissolved before my hungry eyes. "So fresh", "Oh and all homemade" and "such a lot of yummy food", they commented as they passed by plates piled high, as Elaine smiled at me sympathetically.

Up until the earthquakes in 2010 and 2011 we had many luncheons including one where we successfully catered for 70 people, we really slept well that night and so did the bank manager.

Since the quakes visits by seniors groups have tailed off, as did the accommodation but unlike the bed and breakfasts the luncheons have not really picked up again to date. It is a shame as while they were a lot of work we did make some good money on those days and a great deal of satisfaction watching those busy mouths.

Chapter Seven

Shaky Days

As time marches on people tend to forget that there were two major seismic events that rocked Canterbury, the devastating and terrible earthquake, New Zealand's worst natural disaster which occurred in February 2011 and the stronger but less tragic 7.1 magnitude earthquake that woke us at 4.35am on the morning of September 4th 2010.

It had been a long, hard, cold week and I was really looking forward to my Saturday morning sleep-in as we snuggled deep into our cosy warm bed.

Waking from a deep sleep I felt the bed rocking slightly and naturally thought Elaine was rolling over and I put my arm across her for a cuddle, inching open a droopy eyelid to notice the time of 4.35 glowing back at me from my bedside clock radio.

The rocking of the bed started to slowly increase and a faint dull roar started to build and I decided that either Elaine was having a fit, an airliner was about to land on us or we were experiencing an earthquake.

Little did we realize that this was just the start of it, there was still another 44 seconds left to endure. Now, generally 45 seconds is not a great deal of time in the scheme of things however I can quite honestly say that this was the longest three quarters of a minute of my life.

The faint dull roar intensified to a crescendo just as if a 747 was landing inches above us. The bed turned into a very angry wildly bucking bronco and I grabbed hold of Elaine with one arm and grabbed the side of the mattress with the other, told her I loved her and began to make my peace with my maker.

It is amazing what goes through your mind at times like this, an interesting thing to experience, however I would have been more than happy to have given this insight a miss.

I had endured a near death experience a number of years earlier when I nearly drowned as my first born and I were dragged offshore in a rip on an Aussie beach after the lifeguards had gone home. However at the time I was so busy fighting for both our lives that I didn't have time to think about much else.

Forty five seconds though with nothing to do but lie there left me with two options; one was to scream however Elaine was quietly enduring it so I went with option two and reviewed my life to date.

I came to the very satisfying conclusion that I had achieved a lot of what I had wanted to achieve by this stage of my life, our children were healthy and maturing into great people, I was now living a very simple life but in a great environment (hopefully, earthquake notwithstanding) and if these were my last moments in this plane of existence than I was going out cuddled up to the woman I loved and adored.

Not a bad epitaph I decided as I also noticed the bed was slowly coming to a rest, the jet had obviously landed.

As Elaine bounced out of bed to check the kids I glanced again at the clock but it was lost in the darkness. The power was off and everything was inky blackness and eerily still.

I crunched my way up the hall over broken something's all over the floor after hastily throwing on some pants. Elaine had beaten me to the torch and we were all assembling in the lounge room just like a young family on Christmas morning but without the joy.

While the interior of the cottage had been trashed as if our flock of arapawa sheep had taken a short cut through it, the structure appeared to be still hanging together. It would be a couple of hours before day break when we could really assess the damage. I was particularly anxious to check the state of health of our creatures now we knew the family was safe.

We all rugged up against the early morning cold, sitting in candle light listening to reports coming in from the outside world, on a battery powered radio. Like with us, there was not much to report while it was still dark apart from the geo technical details of the massive 7.1 scale earthquake epicentred not too many paddocks away from us.

Dawn arrived at last and after a quick reconnoitre of the farm I was relieved to report that all was well. One of the rabbit hutches had fallen but a nearby tree had gently broken its fall and Cadbury rabbit was fine.

Shiloh, one of our young stud alpaca boys was in an adjoining paddock from the one he had been in at nightfall but his frightened jump was obviously high enough not to do any damage to him or the fence.

What couldn't be noticed at the time though was the effect the quake would have on the fertility of our chickens and rabbits and visitors.

As I returned to the cottage I noticed the two red brick chimneys sitting atop the roof at very creative angles and groaned. The last few years had been a financial nightmare but Elaine thank goodness had been adamant that we must maintain our insurances and how wise she had been.

Of all the places in New Zealand the Canterbury Plains were regarded as one of the least prone areas to a major earthquake. Major fault lines lay under the Southern Alps, on the same system that ran under Auckland and Wellington and ultimately linked New Zealand to the Pacific 'Rim of Fire'

The quietly sleeping Greendale Fault that had lain undetected for thousands of years had chosen our miniscule moment on the planet to roll over into a more comfortable position.

Reviewing the momentous start to the day, any thoughts of my sleep-in now long gone, we all agreed that we had survived it extremely well. On the positive side everyone was at least physically fine, the additions to the cottage on three sides were not as I expected hanging off it and the house appeared perfectly livable though a seriously major clean up was required. The animals were also fine.

On the negative side we had no power, much to our teenage son's chagrin who were eager to log-on, sign-in, load up and rejoin and seek sanctuary in their various virtual worlds.

Actually this did have a positive side as they had no option but to help with the clean up.

Not knowing how long the power was to be off was a worry. While we were able to use the coal range for heating and cooking, without power the pump that supplied the water from our well was not operating so the taps were dry. This was a problem with six humans to hydrate and a serious concern with hundreds of creatures not having water pumped to their various troughs or water containers refilled.

With my befuddled brain still coming to terms with the weird start to the day it took me a minute or two before I remembered the emergency water supply.

A couple of years earlier we had been subjected to a snow storm that had lasted two days and had been ferocious in its intensity. It had taken a whole day to chain saw the fallen trees and huge limbs that had blocked the driveway and our access to the outside world and we had been without power for a few days.

Water had been a major issue then, though fortunately we had had a fewer animals and while we were able to convert snow into water it was not a happy time. I had decided then that from now on we would have some emergency water stored away.

It was to the collection of 20 litre containers of two year old water that I had hidden away at the back of an old shed that I headed for. While the water smelt a bit musty and plasticy it was wet and if used judiciously would hopefully last us for washing and toilet duties and should boil up fine in a billy until the power came back on.

This still left the animals though and they should last a reasonable time consuming what they already had until the water started flowing again. I rejoined Elaine, Bruce and the boys who were busy with the clean up.

The kitchen was probably the worst affected. Our walk-in, step-up door less pantry had virtually exploded and strewn its contents across the kitchen. Flour was mixed with sugar, rice, pasta, spices, cereals and raisins all congealing in a primal soup

83

of sauces and chutneys, pickles, vinegars and cooking oils. "Anyone for breakfast?" I enquired proffering some spoons at the unamused faces looking up at me from the mess.

Bruce was busy at the coal range producing toast as they used to in the old days, mildly charred on one side and with a not unpleasant slightly smokey flavor. The relief on his face was evident, both his beloved television set and his cask of wine had both survived the morning and once the power was back all would be well again in his simple world.

I decided it was time to check out the situation in the Barn. Thank God we had not had guests last night I thought as I walked across the paddock my mind still reeling from the events of the morning so far.

Surely if the cottage had come through relatively unscathed then a corrugated building erected on a concrete base should be fine and I was most relieved to discover that this was indeed the case.

Tentatively stepping through the Barn door I switched on the light remembering immediately that we had no power. There were a few things lying on the floor among the broken china and glass but they were mainly soft craft items and bags of wool and so on. Things appeared to be in pretty good shape over all I decided. The Barn Stay room was pretty much untouched.

Things however were not so good upstairs. Being an avid reader all my life I had over the years accumulated a large number of books across a wide spectrum of subjects.

Twenty five shelves of books that I had last seen in the wall to ceiling bookcases on the walls at the rear of the upstairs office/study/library/overflow accommodation room were lying in a huge heap in front of me. It was as if over the 45 seconds of the earthquake the bookcases had walked themselves into the middle of the room. Proceeded into the centre of the room and then thrown themselves in a tantrum, like a naughty toddler onto the floor taking out gouges of coffee table in the process.

Recruiting one of the clean up crews of boys from the cottage we set about the long task of sorting and clearing up the books. It was as we started to do this rather complicated job, working around large pieces of bookcase that we discovered the sea of small jagged pieces of glass and broken china and wooden ornaments that had been proudly displayed on top of and among the book cases. The glass was predominantly fine crystal which made the clean up even harder and occasionally bloody.

Thinking back now on what a miserable day it was for us all I feel quite humble and our complaints pale into insignificance compared to the absolute horror, devastation and human tragedies that were to take place in just a few months time in Christchurch. We had been so very very lucky and really at the time did not fully appreciate just how lucky we had been. Even now at the time of writing there are still many people waiting on repairs and infrastructure to be rebuilt.

As late morning faded into mid afternoon and with still no power, my thoughts returned to the animals and their water situation while I began my regular rounds of the farm. The adrenaline burst I had experienced earlier was now a distant memory and it had left me starting to feel very weary. However something was able to briefly spark in my brain and I headed over in the direction of the water race hidden away behind the trees and foliage dividing Warwickz Farm from Mc Nasty's dairy farm.

My hunch had been correct, the race which is dry for most of the year still had a quantity of flowing fresh water in it from the recent autumn rains. We may not have power but we did now have water for the animals. The effort it took to ferry many buckets across the paddocks to the troughs was far out weighed by the relief I felt knowing that things were going to all be okay after all.

Power was resumed after 36 hours and life slowly returned to normal, notwithstanding the 20,000 aftershocks we were to endure over the next couple of years.

While the kids were distraught not having access to any plug in devices for the weekend it was Elaine who was most upset as the range of rare breed eggs in the incubator now faced a terminal future.

Being the determined lady she is and refusing to accept anyone's advice about the futility of a rescue mission she set about clucking over them. Fortunately it was a warm and sunny disastrous weekend and Elaine utilized the constructive hand of nature by placing the eggs on the verandah in the sunlight and as it cooled putting them back in the incubator and covering them in alpaca fibre with a plastic sheet over the top and then a blanket.

We were delighted that 5 days later thirteen of the 20 eggs hatched and became affectionately referred to as the *Birthquakers* or the *Tremorloes.*

Due to the February earthquake in Christchurch and the massive call on resources in the region it was to be 20 months later before the $50,000 worth of repairs, including the erection of two ugly industrial looking smoke stacks that replaced our attractive red brick chimneys was completed.

For the repairs to the myriad cracks and fractures that were discovered by the insurance assessors, and the painting and the chimney replacements to take place we were required to vacate the cottage for two weeks.

For most families that would have been a major issue but having the Barn we were able to enjoy a little holiday stay across the paddocks, apart from Bruce who was able to stay in his nearby cabin and sit amongst the repairers dust and debris watching his beloved television in peace in the cottage each evening.

Being a typical staunch Kiwi bloke who tends to deal with his emotions in absolute privacy in case any perceived weakness is exposed, (will us guys never learn?), I was surprised a day later when the power was back on and things were returning to relative normality that a tear did discreetly slide down my cheek.

It was while we were checking our emails, a whole swag of them arrived together from a dozen or so overseas guests we had hosted over the previous few years, some of whom we couldn't even remember.

They were all most concerned about our welfare after the shocking news had made it to their respective countries and

89

wanted to be reassured we were all fine, including the animals, and some even asked it there was anything they could do to help us.

With a pebble in my throat I wiped my tear away and smiled radiantly at Elaine. We had really touched some people's lives and it made us both very, very humble but also very happy in spite of these horrible times.

Chapter Eight

Operation Stoat and Hoglet

One of the rules Elaine and I made at Warwickz Farm is that all
of our creatures which on last count included forty breeds from
20 species, have to be relatively easy to handle and have kind
natures. This makes life easy and pleasant for us and safe for our
visitors and guests.

When I say our creatures I mean the animals and birds that are
here because we arranged it so and do not include the large
variety of animals that make their own decisions where they
want to be, I am of course referring to the wild animals.

Many guests ask how we deal with the likes of foxes and wolves
and snakes and we take delight in advising them that fortunately
New Zealand being an island has no natural predators like these.
This however does not let us off the hook completely as there are

a whole host of introduced nasty little creatures who come to stay from time to time.

Stoats and weasels along with wild cats and rats give us the most grief if we let our guard down. Poultry Lane which is home to most of our rare breed chickens with over twenty various sized and designed chicken coops is like a shopping mall for these unpleasant visitors.

I have visions of them going window shopping while they case the various joints after dark when all is quiet. They stay well hidden during the day for a number of reasons. If they were to attack something the whole of Poultry Lane would erupt in a cacophony of clucking and doodle doing bringing angry faced humans running. If they were more discreet about such an attack the ever watchful duty guinea fowl would let out a raucously loud alarm, warning the off duty guinea fowl of possible danger and alerting the rest of the world in the process. Also the large and slightly fearsome looking Sebastopol geese enjoy a bit of sport and a good chase and are always up for a bit of fun when it arises and a stoat, rat and even a cat would fit the bill.

I am pleased to say that over the years we haven't had too many problems with these predators and that is because we are very wary of them and keep our animal residents in as secure surroundings as possible.

Another contributing factor is the fact that I never want to deal with the mass carnage I discovered one bright sunny spring morning in our earlier days at Warwickz Farm.

Having let out Niki the dog, taken the covers off the guinea pig hutches, replaced the rabbit's overnight water consumption, I then went to let the ducks out of their apartment and finally arrived at the pigeon loft.

The pigeon loft is where our flight of over a dozen white fantail pigeons spend their nights. It is what Elaine refers to as a dilapidated eyesore but what I prefer to consider a rather rustic wooden structure in need of refurbishment.

My first warning that things were not as they should be was when I opened the hatch to the short landing pad the pigeons use for taking off, on their days adventures and landing back on, for some rest and recreation in the evenings. The closeable landing pad was designed to keep these beautiful gentle birds safe from harm during their slumbers. It was odd that there were not at least a couple of pigeons ready to greet the day and waiting on the landing pad doing their pre-flight checks as I approached.

The reason became obvious as I surveyed the scene of carnage through the wire netting frontage. The floor of the loft was littered with the bodies of these lovely creatures.

As the saying goes, 'if you have animals you have death' and we had come to terms that living this closely with nature the cycle of life and death was all part of the rhythm of nature, even the occasional untimely death. However to see such beautiful creatures and so many of them with scarlet splotches around their necks all laying dead and virtually untouched was a shock to the system.

It had to be stoats I decided, dirty rotten little nasty bastards that kill for the sheer joy of it. Injecting their evil yellow fangs into the delicate feathery necks of our pigeons and watching their life drain away before killing another one then another. If there is any animal parallel to humankind's sociopathic psychopath it has to be the stoat, killing for pleasure rather than hunger, clutching their prey in a vice like grip then using their sharp surgical teeth. I felt sick to the stomach and very angry as I began reverently collecting the corpses for quick disposal before anyone else had to witness this tragedy.

On investigation we discovered a small, perfectly round hole in the ground not far from the pigeon loft which I presumed had to be a stoat hole as it was obvious that, tunneling in, had to be the only way they could have got into the loft.

I had not noticed any likely spot that they had got in through, though when I placed a large collection of heavy river stones around the base of the loft the day before. A tunnel set back from the loft was the obvious means of entry and now we had discovered it.

My immediate thought, in mind of restorative justice, was to pour a liberal amount of petrol into the tunnel and toss in a match, one very satisfying whooof and the perpetrator/perpetrators' would be toast and vengeance would be mine.

Elaine quickly reminded me of the dangers of instant retribution and the smouldering smoky remains of the loft that would probably ensue. Not to mention our animal loving conservational credentials.

Death by drowning then, I decided, striding off to fetch a hose. Unfortunately the hose was about two hose lengths short of the nearest water tap so I then went off to get a couple of buckets, large ones.

Fortunately this delay allowed me to calm down some and start thinking a bit more rationally. If I tried to flood them out, I decided then, that there had to be more than a lone ranger, they may just manage to surf their way out to the end of the tunnel, being such devious and cunning little low-lifes and live to kill another day.

I decided that I had better cut off their escape route and, forensically going over the crime scene, like a seasoned detective I located the other end of the tunnel inside the loft which I secured with a very solid rock.

The first dozen or so bucket loads of water that descended down the hole that was about the size of a large walnut, were quite satisfying, even enjoyable as I imagined the little sicko creatures scrambling for their lives against the flood of water.

By the fortieth bucket of water the afternoon was getting longer and I my chores were calling me but I gritted my teeth in grim determination. I had invested too much time, water and emotion to give up now.

By the sixtieth bucket rather than drowning stoats I was drowning out little voices in my head saying "Chris, give it up buddy, you are becoming a little obsessive here, you have animals to feed and it's getting dark', by imagining just how big this tunnel really was.

I truly believe that we had stumbled onto the underground network of a stoat terrorist cell. This was not a tunnel but surely a series of tunnels probably in the process of being dug under many of the chicken coops. It probably had little hollows built into it for resting and nesting and probably birthing more of these little devils.

With the sun starting to set and surrounded by a crowd of on-looking hungry free range chooks and ducks the water cascading from the eighty third bucket started to gurgle back at me from the hole.

After a few moments seeing if the hole was merely suffering from indigestion or was in fact now full I was relieved the see the water level remain constant at ground level.

"Gotya, you little bastards" I sung out in delight as a few close by chooks leapt in the air in fright.

My theory that it was indeed a network of tunnels was confirmed a little later while feeding the chooks along Poultry Lane, when I noticed another damp hole behind one of the chook houses where my deluge had exited.

Nervously I looked around hoping not to find a swampy patch that I had perhaps been watering all afternoon. No, it was all good, Operation Stoat had been a complete success as was officially confirmed in due course as we had no more fatalities' of the evil stoat variety.

I am pleased to report that most of our wild animals tend to give us delight rather than cause temporary mental derangement. One of the more unusual encounters occurred one morning when Bruce decided to feed out some hay to the alpacas in order to give the family staying with us for a couple of days from Hong Kong, a nice experience and photo opportunity.

I joined them noticing how entranced the guests were watching these beautiful and at that time of year heavily fleeced animals gently tucking into a bonus breakfast.

Bruce was slowly wheeling his broken hay bale laden wheel barrow along the race breaking off slices and throwing it across the fence to the patiently waiting alpacas. The hay was gracefully gliding through the air when suddenly this little round grayish lump fell from it and landed on the ground a second later hidden by the newly landed hay.

Not noticing, as he reached for another slice, Bruce repeated the procedure and we all watched in amazement as this time another grayish lump fell to the ground a moment later also covered in hay.

Click click went the cameras and the beaming faced father of the family began to ask me about the additives that were being feed along with the hay. I grabbed Bruce's arm as he reached for another slice and then we gently opened up the bail to discover to everyone's surprise four newly born hedgehogs.

Gently retrieving the recently airborne ones who appeared relatively unscathed and probably thought that they had been born a rather ugly species of bird, we reunited the post natal package into their nest of hay and returned it to the hay barn, intrigued guests in tow to hopefully also reunite them with Ma Hedgehog.

Unfortunately, she had obviously thought her maternal duties had concluded and had made off to parts unknown. We checked every 30 minutes for a couple of hours to see if she had returned but alas she had not, leaving us with somewhat of a dilemma.

"Well, I know we shouldn't interfere with Mother Nature," I said with a sigh to Elaine, "but, well we accidently have and so really we need to try and fix it." I continued looking at the six little creatures nestling in a bowl of straw.

I wouldn't call them exactly cute but they were so tiny I could fit two of them in the palm of my hand and so vulnerable looking with little pixie faces' pink belly's and soft spiny quills all over their backs.

"I've checked it out online and I think we could be on a hiding to nothing, many have tried and few have succeeded" she advised me.

"Nothing ventured, nothing gained," I said with more confidence than I felt "and it would be hard to just abandon them now to a hungry or violent death, hey look," I continued, "I think this one just smiled at me." Pointing at the one I had laying on its back in the palm of my hand all four legs wide as if waiting for a cuddle.

"Oh well, I hope you know what you're taking on." Elaine said returning to her monitor for more information.

Every six hours over the next two days we were busy, (me in the hours of darkness) mixing various milk formulas and patiently syringing it down their tiny throats. We then had to palpate all six of their little bellies after each feed until they successfully did their sticky little bits of business. It brought back memories of the kids when they were small and messy.

Unfortunately, probably due to a lack of colostrum from their runaway mother they slowly, after the second day, passed on, one after another leaving us though sad, but also enriched by a wonderful experience few people are lucky enough to enjoy.

We are sure our guests from Hong Kong enjoyed going home with a most unique experience to share with their friends. I was just pleased that they were not staying with us and observing Operation Stoat at its most manic stages when we were dealing with a creature at the other end of the vulnerability range.

Chapter Nine

Wild Encounters

A number of wild creatures have charmed, entertained and amazed us over the years and one of the earlier ones was Mortie the Vole.

We have a policy of not allowing wild guests in the Red Barn nor wild creatures to become guests on Warwickz Farm. However, like with most rules there is always the exception, Mortie became an exception.

It was a sunny summer's day and Elaine and I after a nice lunch of salad sandwiches filled full of our beautiful sweet and juicy home grown tomatoes, decided to visit the new additions to Poultry Lane, a couple of young Silver Sebright bantam chickens that had arrived the day before.

Sebrights are a very rare breed named after Sir John Sebright who was instrumental in the development of the breed at the turn of the 18th century. He crossed the Laced Polish fowl with bantams in an attempt to replicate the beautiful plumage of the Laced Polish chicken on as small a bird as possible.

It took him twenty years to finally achieve his goal the two beautiful Silver Sebright specimens we had before us, with their beautiful fine black lacework on their small white bodies.

However over this long period of inter breeding and crossing he unfortunately bred all their nurturing instincts out of them so now they lay few eggs, will not sit on them and if you incubate the eggs for them and proudly deliver the hatchlings to them they will attack them. It is no wonder these beautiful chooks are a rare breed.

Like all successful people Sir John, once the Silver Sebrights were on the ground, reset his goals and it was not too long before the even more eye catching Gold Sebright arrived. It was not many months later that we took on the gold's, with their beautiful lacework set against a feathery background of deep gold colouring.

So, we were busy admiring our new feathered friends when we noticed this little rodent quite happily standing in the coop as if he too was enjoying a relaxing Sunday afternoon. Opening the door we expected it to quickly dart away to safety but instead it stayed exactly where it was watching us with interest.

When I reached in, now fully expecting an urgent retreat, it remained still and while not actually climbing into my hand made no fuss when I picked it up and with a grin offered it to Elaine who quickly backed away.

The small little fellow sat quite comfortably in my palm as we went to show the boys and Bruce. After repeated pleas to keep him we reminded the boys of the farm rules regarding wild creatures and we placed him nice and safely in a lush paddock far away from his feathered friends and left him to his life.

Later that afternoon as I approached the Sebright coop, while feeding the chooks along Poultry Lane, I wondered how the funny looking little mouse with the round ears was faring. Moments later I was able to ask him as he was back where we

106

found him sitting happily between the two slightly bemused looking Sebrights.

He was a determined looking fellow who had travelled a fair distance on his tiny legs in search of his new friends. Obviously a social animal in need of company we decided to let the boys have their wish and set him up in a comfortable cage in the younger boy's room where he was christened Mortie.

Intrigued as to what he officially was with his dark colouring and roundish ears we did some research and discovered that he was a vole, commonly known as a field mouse, though not actually a mouse at all.

Belonging to the genus *Microtus* there are 240 varieties in the vole group including lemmings and muskrats we discovered. We thought it was most fitting that some of Warwickz Farm wildlife also included different and intriguing creatures.

It did not take long for this tiny creature to start growing. In fact he was eating so much and getting so big after a few weeks that we thought there may be a problem. We discovered though that voles can eat the equivalent of their body weight in 24 hours. He was not quite the cute little fellow anymore that had so enchanted us.

In the interests of his heart health we provided him with a treadmill for his cage so he could burn off some of his excess weight at the same time reconsidering whether we should have broken our rule about wild creatures after all.

Mortie started to become pretty manic on his treadmill with the boys complaining about the constant humming coming from the cage all hours of the day and night.

I idly suggested to Elaine that maybe we could somehow harness the energy he was generating, perhaps power the boy's room and sell the excess back to the main grid. An unimpressed Elaine told me that Mortie was becoming scary and might have to go.

Looking down at Mortie, now a dark furry ball of energy we asked the boys what they thought about releasing him back to the wild so they could have their nice quiet room back. They not so reluctantly agreed and Jody reached in to the cage to pick him up.

With a yelp Jody stepped back as Mortie, having buried his teeth into Jody's finger, now made a break for it and landed with a loud plop on the floor. Before anyone could react he had scaled the curtains like a mountaineer on speed and was skillfully running along the top of the curtain railing before stopping to catch his breath.

Having honed my animal catching and recapturing skills over the years I grabbed a wastepaper basket with one hand, emptying its contents all over the floor and grabbing the curtains swung them up and over Mortie and bundled the portion I hoped Mortie was caught up in, into the bin, calling out for someone to get me Bruce's welders leather gloves.

Moments later we had Mortie the vole clutched tightly in the teeth proof gloves and on his way to the furthest boundary of the farm as per Elaine's who was busy doctoring to Jody's finger, instructions.

As I said farewell to this once delightful rodent it occurred to me that destiny had forewarned us of this fateful outcome. We had named him Mortie the Vole which was pretty damn close to that famous fictional master of evil Vole De Mort.

Some of our interactions with wild animals have been quite short lived encounters including the time I came across an opossum fossicking under the oak trees near the guinea pig hutches at the back of the gardens.

Possums are nocturnal creatures and apart from road kill are rarely seen in the daytime so I was quite surprised to see this obviously confused or perhaps sick one and hastened inside to grab my video camera.

Quietly returning I very slowly approached it, not wanting to scare it off but wanting to get close enough for some good footage.

It was a little on the smaller side of average and had a thick brownish black pelt and after a bit more fossicking among the golden autumn leaves it began to turn towards me. I froze, trying to blend in with the background hoping not to startle it and watch it race away.

To my amazement it stared right at me and made no attempt to flee. Inching forward I was still expecting it to make an urgent break for cover when as I came closer I noticed its pink unseeing eyes looking through me, not at me.

The possum's snout was sniffing frantically though as it sensed that something had entered its environment that was foreign and most likely a threat to it.

After a good minute or so of aiming my lens at him as we stared each other down I decided that a bit more action was needed for my documentary film so I again started inching forward.

I got closer to him than I expected before I elicited a response and that was his instinctive inbuilt alarm to shinny up the nearest tree and out of danger.

According to his security defense system the nearest horizontal object showing treelike characteristics was me and he then

111

attempted to scurry his way up my trouser leg propelled by his very sharp claws.

Like all intrepid documentary makers I filmed for as long as was painfully possible before politely explaining by way of wildly kicking legs that I was in fact not a tree.

He then scurried away in the opposite direction and my lens followed his descent high into the nearest official tree, an old oak.

The family derived many moments of viewing pleasure watching the video, especially the jerky shots of leaves sky and legs that was accompanied by a soundtrack of unmanly-like yelps and curses.

Two days later I sadly discovered my furry film star buddy laying by the side of the highway, staring up at me with his pink eyes, a victim of his sensory deprivation and faulty security defense system.

We have our share of seasonal visitors from the wild like the pair of blue heron who nest at the very top of the highest pine tree behind the hay barn every year and delight us with their graceful gliding on the thermal wind currents way above us.

The swallows following their amazingly long trip from the northern hemisphere appear to take great pleasure in flying round and around the Red Barn every year before returning to their mud nest we discovered one day built under a collapsed edge of the earth bank bordering the water race.

A native New Zealand wood pigeon, a kereru, before the earthquakes, was another regular visitor. This large magnificent looking bird used to spend a couple of weeks feasting on the nectar from our kowhai trees and getting drunk on the over ripe plums on the wild plum trees bordering the farm.

The kereru mysteriously always arrived alone each year but was obviously a sociable bird as for most of the time it was here it really wanted to hang out with our fantail pigeons.

Being so much larger than our pigeons all it managed to do with its friendly fly-bys was to terrify and intimidate them.

They would take off as a flock and settle somewhere farther afield and sometimes if the overtures continued somewhere much farther afield. We had once seen a hawk dramatically take out one of our pigeons that was flying quite high, like an air to air missile so they were very wary of larger birds in their air space.

We wondered whether this alienation had made the poor thing take solace in the fermenting plums.

As mentioned previously we are always alert to any possible threats to our creatures and one of our methods is to use rat traps. But this day it was not a rat we caught.

One of these traps lies between a couple of the coops on Poultry Lane and is a long rectangular plastic structure with a ramp that the dastardly rat walks up to retrieve the bait, which is at the other end behind a metal observation grill. As the rat reaches the top of the ramp it over balances and drops down allowing the rat access to the bait but no means of escape.

As I walked along the Lane one day I had a feeling that I was being watched, as if eyes were following my every move. Seeing nothing I continued on my way but still couldn't lose that eerie feeling of being observed. On further investigation I discovered a baby wild rabbit while exploring its new world had decided to investigate the bait and was lucky that I happened to have passed.

It was only, I guessed five or six weeks old and retrieving it from the trap I held it tightly in my hands. It did not appear to be in any great distress apart from the fact that it was being gripped by an ugly furless monster.

Being used to handling our variety of trusting rabbits I had to remember to keep a firm grip on it as trudging across the farm I decided to release it across the border to the relative safety of Mcnasty's dairy farm.

A fairly recent incident involving wild birdlife happened early last summer but in a slightly more domestic setting than usual.

The barbeque area that I mentioned earlier is under cover and there is a large sideboard set up along one wall adjacent to the dining area. The sideboard is used for plates cutlery and so on and on its several shelves are a variety of vases and pottery jars and sundry knick knacks.

Having picked up either a knick or a knack that had fallen from it on to the ground I idly mentioned it in passing to Elaine. She informed me that this had been happening a lot recently and something must be getting up there and dislodging them.

Concerned about the safety of particularly the lovely pottery jars and thinking maybe the opossums we occasionally hear lurking past our adjacent bedroom window were the culprits, I decided further investigation was merited.

Everything seemed in order, I couldn't detect any possum droppings and so I stood back to review the situation. It was then that I heard the very soft sweet sound of hatchlings chirping.

I quickly traced the sound to a large, orange, pottery jar with a wide body tapering to a narrow neck, the type of thing you would find in an ancient pyramid I imagine. At the bottom of which, nestled in some straw, I found four bright yellow french horn type instruments attached to pinky bodies emitting this high pitched and rather urgent peeping sound. Four newly hatched starlings were waiting to be fed.

This was the most interesting nest I had discovered so far and certainly the safest and warmest. I decided to settle back in a chair and very quietly wait for mother starling to arrive. Judging from the urgency of her babes she couldn't be far away.

No more than ten minutes later she arrived, her mouth laden with a succulent wriggling morsel and carefully positioning herself for a helicopter style landing and only just missing hitting a wooden pepper grinder, she disappeared into the jar.

I congratulated myself on having the presence of mind to stay and await this curious event and then cursed myself for not having the presence of mind to make sure I had the video camera with me!

We decided it was best to leave them where they were for now and for the next three weeks we maximised the situation and it became a highlight of the farm tours as I brought the guests over to the jar and let them marvel at these fast growing birds.

The day duly arrived though when they were fully feathered and the jar smelled particularly funky that they had to leave home and venture off into the wide wonderful world. Normally mother would nudge them out of the nest and as they fell their wings would open and the miracle of flight would be experienced for the first time. However as they were deep in the bottom of a jar this was not an option.

After waiting until they had been fed and mother was still in the vicinity I reached in and scooped them out one by one and they jumped out of my open hand and with wildly flapping wings each of them crashed into a nearby hedge. Five minutes later mother starling had them assembled and they were last seen flapping and fluttering away high up into the oak trees.

I watched them fly away with mixed emotions, not realising how fond I had become of them and how the tours would lose something now they had gone. Then I smiled to myself as I thought how lucky I was and of how few people in their workaday life would have been able to share such an intimate experience with a family of starlings.

Chapter Ten

Harvest Time

Living off the smell of an oily rag over the years we are always looking at ways to maximise opportunities that Warwickz Farm provides particularly in an area close to my heart, food.

We are blessed by a large number of wild plum trees that grow along the banks of the water race that divides us from Mc Nasty's dairy farm. We have been told that some of these trees could be extremely old and most years they provide us with a bountiful harvest of fruit.

Being rare breed animal farmers it wasn't long before we became interested in what I suppose could be termed rare breed food.

Just as it is important for people to continue to preserve the old breed animal gene pool to ensure that in the future, if mankind gets too clever in the relentless pursuit of the economic exploitation of animals and some disaster occurs, requiring mankind to go back to the original recipe and start again, then we will still have some of the original ingredients, so too with food and seeds.

Heritage seeds and the cultivation and propagation of them is something Warwickz Farm will be focusing on even more in the future, but let me get back down from my soap box and back to the plums.

The plum seeds from a variety of trees must over time have flowed along the water race and as the waters receded they propagated along its banks.

We have identified three different strains, all having quite small fruit, more the size of a very large cherry than a plum. Some are more red than purple and the flesh of one is quite waxy and all are sweet, juicy and delicious.

Apart from sharing them with the kereu, the trees are quite high and about 80 percent of the fruit is inaccessible except to birds but I make sure we get our fair share of the pickings. Elaine

121

waves her magic kitchen ladle and turns them into mouth watering jams and sauces and chutneys and pies and I am starting to get hungry so I will now finish the list.

A good percentage of her creations, unfortunately for me, end up for sale to guests and after sampling them, there are not many who go away without something tasty to enjoy on the rest of their travels.

Our harvest this last season was a little different to most, the fruit arriving late, maturing quickly and disappearing particularly fast, even our portion on the lower limbs.

We had been pretty busy with guests and tours over the period and I had been trying to find some time to collect a couple of buckets for Elaine to morph into yummies and I had noticed across the paddock that the did seem to be rapidly disappearing. Later that sunny afternoon I made some time to liberate some of them and as I approached the back of the paddock I discovered the reason for our fast shrinking supply of plums.

Tracey, our mischievous angora/saanen goat was reaching up on her hind legs, grabbing a mouthful of branch and shaking it for all she was worth. I am sure I detected a goatish smile on her face as letting go of the branch the last of the showering multitude of plums cascaded to the ground all around her.

I then watched, hands on my hips, as she proceeded to scarf the whole lot of them before gazing dreamily, tree ward at the purplish jewels glistening in the sunlight and returning to another likely spot and repeating the procedure.

Not only had the mystery of the disappearing plums been solved but also something Bruce and I had noticed and had pondered on and that was the large collections of bleached plum stones we had found in various places all over the paddock – plums recycled through Tracey.

Over the years we had learnt through hard experience that you had to get up very early in the morning if you wanted to outwit a goat. For this reason I decided, as I headed off to look for a

123

tarpaulin, not to try to keep Tracey away from the plums but rather learn from her and attempt to beat her at her own game.

Returning with a couple of buckets and a tarp I ran Tracey away towards the lesser laden trees to continue her work and laid the tarp on the ground under my large tree and leapt up to grab a couple of heavy branches.

I experienced the same delight Tracey obviously had as I was bombarded by a shower of small, soft, sweet succulent bombs of sun kissed plums. Like Tracey I began scarfing them before my human instincts returned and I began loading the buckets like the hunter gatherer of old that I had become.

I had evened the score with Tracey and over the next couple of weeks, between us, Tracey with her regular but small tree shaking and me with my infrequent but monster tree shaking managed to maximise the remains of the harvest to the satisfaction of all. Well, perhaps maybe not the nervous smaller birds in the higher branches, but hey, that's just life.

A number of years ago we cajoled Bruce who is a natural at building things, much better than me, to put together a sizeable tunnel house made from recycled lengths of six metre plastic piping, a massive roll of plastic sheeting and some old lumber Elaine and I had scrounged from somewhere.

In a television deprived flurry of creative activity of which he is very good at but alas most infrequently, we had a tunnel house that was to keep us in fresh vegetables and tomatoes and save us a great deal of money over the years.

The tomatoes especially were amazing, old heritage seeds produced the biggest, juiciest, sweetest and tastiest ones we had ever enjoyed. Those that were not used for meals Elaine turned into sauces and soups and chutneys, some we sundried and any surplus was either sold or given away to friends.

I remember slicing up some samples for visitors enjoying a luncheon one afternoon and piled a collection of generous sized plastic bags full of these tempting delights with the samples on a nearby table with a sign offering them for sale at $1.00 a bag.

As the diners were coming back with their second helping of desserts I addressed them about our bountiful harvest of tomatoes and turned around to point to the bulging bags and tempting samples only to be surprised to see that the slices were gone and the bags had already been replaced by piles of coins. Turning back to the sea of smiling faces I offered to find more if anyone had missed out.

To be fair to Bruce, he was pretty proud of his tunnel house and decided to utilise his green fingers to grow a variety of lettuces, cucumbers, courgettes, pumpkins and gherkins as well as the tomatoes over time.

The tunnel house is close to the cottage but is actually located in the paddock with the Gotland and other sheep and Pinot our aging angora buck.

Pinots more recent name has been the Unihorn or Unihorner since he got into a butting competition with Harry the famous tunneling Gotland ram. He obviously lost the contest to the un-horned Harry; Gotland rams do not have horns; however they

126

must have very hard heads as Pinot's left horn was snapped off at the base leaving Pinot most bemused and now twice as hard to catch.

Angora bucks horns are quite magnificent, similar to the Texas longhorn cattle, with a wide sweeping handlebar appearance, so it was quite a blow to the ego of the old fellow. I was no longer feeling sorry for him however a couple of months later in mid summer when I quickened my pace with mounting alarm towards the tunnel house as I noticed the door that had been left open to the world.

The alarm fast turned to grief and then despair as I surveyed the total devastation inside the tunnel house. The dozen or so large plastic buckets that had held the thick green foliage of the tomato plants laden with dozens of variously green and orange tinged fruit had been skittled like a row of pins in a bowling alley, the limbs trodden underfoot and most of the tomatoes consumed.

The small pumpkins, courgettes and cucumbers had been separated from the vines and lay in various stages of destruction and the range of fancy lettuces were hardly recognisable in the green tangle covering the ground. There amongst all this green debris was a peacefully sleeping bulging gutted one horned angora buck.

I must confess, and this for an animal lover, let alone a rare breed animal farmer, is hard to do, I allowed my anger to exit through my body via my gumboot as it, not in a gentle manner, nudged Pinot awake, seconds before he shot back out the door allowing my grief to return.

Fortunately we still had our original vegetable garden to fall back on, with its potatoes and carrots, spinach and broccoli. We also had another pumpkin patch where we had been experimenting with heritage pumpkin seeds.

One of the most sensational pumpkins we produced was quite small and bright yellow and had a series of ribs along its exterior. Not only did it have a very nice nutty flavour to it, it was also a visual delight with its bright colouring and when sliced it resembled bright yellow cogs which certainly enhanced the dining experience.

Another pumpkin variety we had, wrapped its vines around the lower limbs of an apple tree which resulted in a couple of very large light green pumpkins defying gravity by hanging in the air like enormous genetically engineered apples to the scariest degree. Both these and the cog pumpkins ended up featuring in our Warwickz Farm newsletter that we also publish on the website.

The summer months see my striding along the water race covered in long red lacerations with a bucket fast filling up with juicy blackberries. It never fails to amaze me how the biggest fattest most tantalisingly mouthwatering ones are always about half an arms length away from where you can safely and comfortably reach them from. It also never fails to amaze me that I will quite happily endure intense moments of pain in order to feed my craving to have them.

Unfortunately last season's blackberry bounty was severely reduced as McNasty had decided to spray this tasty noxious weed. About five percent of it grows on the banks bordering his side of the boundary and his cows cannot even get close to it so I don't know why he was worried and I suppose he thought we wouldn't mind if he sprayed ours as well.

I did manage to get some revenge as the seasons changed however by ducking under his hot electric fence and liberating some huge and delicious meadow mushrooms growing not far away on his lush pasture.

Our very old walnut tree that shares the paddock with Tracey and the ducks and the hay barn has given us some wonderful harvests of these delicious nuts. It took a few years though to realise that while we had a walnut tree that had fruit, why it was that it never really made it to the kitchen. This was because there is more to collecting walnuts than just collecting walnuts; well this is the case on Warwickz Farm anyway.

First of all the nuts will fall from the tree, you know the ones, those round browny ball-shaped things with the hard shells. Well, that's not what falls from our tree; our walnuts arrive in thick green fleshy packaging that eventually turns into a brown soggy pulp and rots away leaving the ball shaped thing as described above.

Unless you notice these green round things amongst the other green things like grass, leaves and so on then creatures like horses and donkeys will crunch them underfoot or opossums will scoff them before you are even aware they are there.

Once you are onto this you can then begin collecting the green walnuts and storing them somewhere sheltered where they can dry out and shed their green skins. You decide that somewhere outside close to the tree, for convenience, would be ideal; somewhere the fresh air and sun can naturally dry them out. That is precisely what the possums hope you are thinking.

Returning with new green walnuts to add to your collection you think it a little odd that the collection doesn't appear to be

131

increasing in size and eventually wise up that possums have located your cache in the old cooking pot you left on top of the stump under the trees by the gate.

Realising how silly you have been you then find an old onion bag to allow the air to circulate freely and hang the bag from a tree only to discover on your next visit that a hole has been bitten through the bottom of said onion bag and you have no more walnuts at all.

You eventually clue up to the fact that you need to store them in a warm dry place not outdoors and find a suitable shed. Once you have replenished your supply, if still available, you then assist the drying process by removing the brown soggy mess from the hard shell and discover that walnuts are a source of a very strong and able black dye which you then showcase to the world with your fingers over the next month or so.

Once the remaining walnuts are dry you can then shell them, a process that gets easier over the days as you discover there are easier ways then smashing them and their meaty contents to smithereens with a hammer.

At the end of the section you are left with a small jarful of very tasty walnuts and now realise why they are so expensive in the supermarkets.

If you have used your head you have also discovered a wonderful new natural dye which you then dilute and into various shades of black and dark browns and distil for your very clever wife to use to dye the fibres and wools she uses in her creations.

As I say, nothing gets wasted if possible on Warwickz Farm.

Our community of 20 or so guinea pigs requires constant feeding to keep their little metabolisms ticking over especially the younger ones. Most of their hutches have fine wire netting at the base of the uncovered section so they can access grass and ever fresh grass as we move the hutches round regularly.

Well, that is the case during the spring and autumn seasons when there is plenty of green growth, however summer and winter are not so easy and I have to somehow come up with a daily large sack of the green stuff otherwise spend a fortune on shop bought guinea pig pellets and a fortune we do not have available.

You may remember McNasty's huge irrigator that so enraged me as it sucked dry our old well, well I am pleased to say we have it working for us with regards to feeding the guinea pigs. Or we have until he gets to read this book.

Due to the curvature in a couple of places of the water race McNastys industrial sized watering can overlaps the race and even in the driest months we have enough lush growth of grass and water cress to tide us over.

In fact it is quite a pleasant task collecting the daily sack of grass in summer. The race when empty is about 5 foot below ground level and due to its age the abundance and variety of vegetation and berries and wild ducks and pukekos make it a charming place for a stroll.

It is also quite amusing when some of the dairy cows come to investigate the movement along the race and you look up into their huge black and white faces with their sad looking soulful

eyes. Not so amusing is when you go to grab a huge handful of

long bladed grass only to shriek in pain as a lone jagged

blackberry vine buried deep amongst it rips your hand to shreds.

Oh the joys and woes of living in the country.

Chapter Eleven

The Tour

Over the years we have enjoyed playing host to literally hundreds of people from all around the world since our very first one from the South Pole. Most of our guests have stayed for a one night bed and breakfast visit, though many have enjoyed longer farm stays and we have accommodated the occasional contractor, working locally for longer stays over the winter months.

The big difference with a stay at Warwickz Farm is that you not only enjoy a comfortable bed in lovely surroundings followed by a sumptuous breakfast but you are also offered the farm tour.

We have been delighted to discover that the tour has become somewhat legendary among some of our guests who have insisted their friends come and stay and enjoy the tour; others have waxed lyrical about it in our guest book and online blogs.

The shortest tour I have led took forty five minutes with the longest taking four and a half hours. They vary depending on the amount of interest shown and time restraints due to onward travel. The average tour lasts around two and a half hours.

In fact the tours and their popularity, with the very many passionate stories of our animals and life on the farm became the inspiration for this book, allowing us to share our wonderful experiences with you dear reader and a much wider audience.

So, let's go on a quick tour. The Warwickz Farm tour generally commences after breakfast after I have collected any leftover slices of the thick and crunchy country style toast and liberated a large leafy pile of weeping willow leaves.

First stop is in front of the Barn where we meet Nova the once orphan lamb who leads her family up to the fence to cadge any food on offer. The Gotland Pelt sheep arrive at a trot when they notice the gathering.

Occasionally, when they are on the other side of the paddock I will wander over with some willow branches until the flock sees me and races me back to the fence line, as I do an impersonation of a farmer being chased by a bull, to the delight of our guests.

Next we visit the alpacas grazing adjacent to and behind the Barn. These very curious creatures cautiously approach us and stick out their elegant long necks to sample the proffered willow leaves.

Being such exotic creatures few guests are familiar with them so we bring them up to speed on this charming breed of camelid. The fact that these very clean animals only do their business in certain places as outlined by the piles of chocolate drops always raises a smile.

Approaching the kunekune pig paddocks is one of my favourite moments of the tour. Quite often Robbie and Rosie will be asleep on the opposite side of the paddock. Once I have everybody watching I call their names and immediately they both spring to their feet and come bounding over to greet us like large happy puppies.

They are rewarded with the slices of toast I salvaged from the breakfast tray and wolf them down as I relate the interesting history of the breed and our special kunekune moments. Patience dear reader you will be catching up with them in a later chapter.

By now we have reached Poultry Lane and having just visited the ham we then get to meet the hens that lay the green eggs, the arucauna chooks. They are a lavender coloured chicken that hail from South America and yes, the eggs have an either faint green of slightly bluish tinge to them but taste just like any other egg.

We then review the different breeds of chicken including Chinese silkies, Sebrights, pekins, rhode island reds, buff orpingtons, old English games, bantam leghorns and so on.

Halfway down the lane we duck into Tracey Goats paddock to feel her soft mohair fleece and say hi to the rare breed ducks and Sebastopol geese. It is here that I explain why Tracey has got her own paddock and is tethered to a tyre that she tows around behind her.

Tracey's mother Lacey passed on when she was only 2 days old and I got the job of bottle feeding her and so it was me she bonded with in her formative years. As she regards me as her mother she tends to want to be close to me and as she is a goat and hence has no respect for fences, gates and so on and with the gardens being liberally sprinkled with plants that are toxic to goats we needed to put her in the most secure paddock.

After several arduous occasions of having to find Tracey miles down the water race and then manhandle her across barb wired fences we thought it wise to trail her tyre along behind her. This way she has freedom of movement but once over a fence she is anchored there until the cavalry arrive.

The remainder of Poultry Lane is completed with guests learning about our intriguing critically endangered Royal Palm Turkeys and meeting a variety of free range poultry dancing around us looking for a handout.

Pedro the donkey and Fernando the miniature horse are waiting for us at the end of the Lane in the Jenny Craig paddock.

140

We quickly reassure our tourists that the paddock should not be taken as an indication that we are treating these equine buddies cruelly; in fact the opposite is the case.

Donkeys, ponies and miniature horses have what seems like uncontrolled appetites and probably like me, will eat whatever is available to them. This is not good though as they will eventually founder, that is fall to the ground and well, sometimes they don't get up again. Unlike me, who has never had any trouble getting up again after a good feed.

Pedro came to us due to a marriage break up and with neither partner able to take him along on their new lives their loss was certainly our gain.

He is a pure white English donkey with a lovely nature and we use him to educate people about differences between donkeys and horses and ponies and that while they might have long faces they are generally happy creatures and make great friends.

Donkeys have a reputation for being stubborn and usually not too bright and we quickly debunk this myth by relating a couple

141

of incidents including one about the time I tested Pedro's suitability to have children on his back.

Elaine is a firm believer in the maxim that prevention is better than cure and when I first suggested that it would be nice for children to have donkey rides she was naturally nervous about the concept.

"The last thing we need is for some poor kid to fall off him and hurt himself." She lamented

"He should be fine", I insisted, "you shouldn't worry, he's such a nice natured thing." I continued.

"I can just see the headline. **'Warwickz Farm Farm Sued By Parents of Child Seriously Hurt By Fall from Nice Natured Donkey'**." She said.

It was such a nice idea though and offered us the chance to earn perhaps a few extra dollars, so it was decided that if I could prove he could handle having children on his back without testing the theory with live children the idea could go ahead.

142

I determined that if Pedro could take my weight on his broad back without any trouble than a child on his back would be a breeze. I grabbed a horse blanket and made make shift reins out of binder twine and braced myself for my first donkey ride.

As I gently eased my not insignificant frame onto his back and felt Pedro's hoofs sink softly deeper into the paddock, Pedro was left with somewhat of a dilemma. If he bucked me off which he probably considered then he would be deemed a stubborn animal and if he just let me sit astride him and refused to further exert himself to carry me forward as per my command he would be deemed dumb.

Pedro, like all donkeys, being neither stubborn nor dumb, decided on a course of action that would result in his immediate comfort without their being any unpleasant consequences to him.

He proceeded to slowly but steadily carry me towards the huge macrocarpa hedge and as he went under it I was left with the choice of either sliding off him or being forced off as the lower lying branches of the hedge levered me off. The choice was mine not his; he was quite content either way.

Duly sliding off I chuckled to myself at his wisdom but wanted to confirm it wasn't just down to chance and so repeated the procedure twice more with the same result. It was in fact a win win situation, I had proved that he could carry me safely and steadily, though I was far too heavy for him and he had proved that he was neither stubborn nor dumb.

The tour continues into the gardens along a leafy pathway past the Chinese and Japanese quails and sundry free ranging chickens and Jaspar Parrot, named after a famous English comedian with a very similar name. Jaspar is an Indian Rose Neck parrot and is still quite young, not having earned his ring yet and still unable to speak English. I hope to train him to say as people go by "screech screech move along, nothing to see, move along, nothing to see, screech, screech". Elaine often wonders about my sense of humour.

The end of this pathway leads us to our main rabbitry, home to a number of cute bunnies currently including Flemish Giants, Netherland dwarfs, minilops, and a mini rex.

Hugo, named because he is humungous is the Flemish Giant rabbit that first greets our tourists and he quite happily cuddles up to anyone who wants to, or is big enough to, give this big boy a hug. His long body covered in fawn fur is very soft and he is treated like a teddy bear come to life.

Bella, like Bonny before her, the exquisite blue Netherland Dwarf, exhibits the other end of the range, the smallest breed of rabbit. She sits happily in the palm of my hand, her tiny ears barely twitching as entranced visitors' stroke, prod and poke her. Her face looks just like a little grey squirrel.

Cadbury the mini rex is very old and a bit grumpy as I keep a firm hold of her as our tourists marvel at her fur, that resembles crushed velvet so much so that it changes to a deeper tone of chocolate when the fur is stroked the wrong way. I always get a laugh when they discover this chocolate coloured bunny is called Cadbury.

The mini lops are always very popular with their compact plump bodies and floppy down ears and like Bella, most of them sit happily in the palm of my hand to entertain their new friends. They are the breed we sell most of for pets due to their cuteness, size and gentle natures.

One of our favourite times is when baby rabbits are born. The first week they are bald and blind and helpless, the second week they have fur and this second, the third and fourth week they double their size each week. I start handling them from week two as firstly I cannot resist and secondly, being handled so early makes them so much tamer and calmer and much quicker to train. Unfortunately since the earthquakes we are not experiencing this joy as often as we like to.

Teasing our tourists about shortly going to meet the world's rarest bunnies, the Enderby Island rabbit, we continue our walk through the gardens, across an old wooden bridge and emerge onto the front lawn of the cottage, once through the nearby pergola we are surrounded by a multitude of guinea pig hutches. Once we arrive a chorus of weep weep weeping usually occurs as the observant little creatures hope I have with me one of my yummy sacks of grass.

Currently the guinea stars are Pikachu, the elderly, large sable guinea with a very long 1970s style glam rock haircut who was returned to us, as his new young owner had decided not to look after him, and his mother decided to return him. He sits in my hand like the wise old man on the mountaintop.

A couple of 4 month old Peruvian guineas are the flavour of the season, probably because they resemble expensive shop bought fluffy toys, batteries not required. You cant help but touch these little cuties who seem to enjoy it a much as the visitors.

Goldie the fully grown Peruvian is another star, who when we have pre school groups usually along with Pikachu has to endure the humiliation of Elaine plaiting them and having bows and hair clips attached to them to the smiles and delight of the little people.

"Oh come on Chris," Elaine says to me, "the kids love it and so do the guineas, you old stick in the mud".

"Err Elaine," I say, "these are guys you're doing this to you know." I continue as the guineas and I look at each other in exasperation.

Goldie is always fun to get out of his hutch as when I open one end he dives into a plastic pipe tunnel on the outside end and hides and always seems so surprised when I reach in for the tunnel and pluck him out of it like a magician to the delight of our visitors.

Other guineas we introduce include merinos that have a thick coarse coat which in winter often has crimp similar to that found in sheep. We also have Abyssinians with the lovely rosettes set into their fur and rexes the short haired guineas.

The opportunity to stroke the firmly held Enderby Island rabbits and hear their story of evolution and possible extinction is also greeted with enthusiasm and interest before we say hi to nearby Sassy or Cybil (depending on who is on duty), two Chinese silkie chickens who are both real characters.

Both chickens happily pose for photographs with our visitors either sitting on my or a brave tourists shoulder or head to the applause and the clicking of cameras.

Both chickens have from time to time enjoyed much of a tour perched on my shoulder and whenever I need to put them down so I can showcase another creature they will stay where they are put, for as long as it takes, to the surprise of the visitors.

Occasionally however, the tour has continued with them forgetfully being left behind and a couple of times I have gone back guiltily to find them still patiently waiting a long time after the tour has concluded.

Sassy and Cybil are a unique part of the team and also help sometimes with meetings and greetings. It is also relaxing when not working just to stroll around the farm with one of them perched atop a shoulder like a one eyed pirate's parrot. Sassy also has other important duties that you will discover soon.

The tour concludes as we brush past the herb garden briefly stopping to sniff the wonderful pineapple mint with a look through the interesting items on display in the Red Barn.

The Gotland fleece that I ripped off a relieved Hermione's back is a feature, the famous sheepskin without a skin. Visitors, after seeing all the animals can now relate really well to the the raw fibres and wools and the carded fibres and yarns in the variety of natural colours and then hopefully decide to purchase some of the lovely creations fashioned out of them.

The culmination of the tour is the viewing of Elaine's two very special quilts that need to be viewed from a distance. We have our visitors line up in the race and then show them the quilts made up of many small squares in a range of colours with no discernible rhyme nor reason to the design.

As we march backwards the quilts slowly come to life, the further back we go the more distinct they become. We know when we have moved far enough back as that is when the cheer goes up and the frowns disappear and they can see the alpaca in the paddock in one and the close up of a cats face in the other.

The small squares of fabric represent pixels as in a digital image and the photos the quilts are made from come to life with digital clarity. A glance through a cameras viewfinder immediately reads the image so we discourage photos until afterwards.

If you would like to know how these amazing quilts are made then all you have to do is "Come on a tour and we will tell you." Says Elaine.

Chapter Twelve

Be Our Guest

On entering the tourism industry as a hospitality provider, one would expect it to be a lovely way to earn a living while at the same time meeting a range of interesting and diverse guests from around the world. Realistically though you would expect to meet a certain percentage of people whose acquaintance you would not pursue in normal circumstances.

The incredible thing is, to date; we have yet to have a guest we would not welcome back. I have pondered this situation from time to time and come to the conclusion that because of what we have to offer on Warwickz Farm, the animals, the crafts, the gardens and the chance for time out from the hustle and bustle of modern life we attract likeminded people who appreciate all of the above. I believe generally, animal lovers and crafts people tend to be kind and gentle folk.

Having concluded all of the above, a family from Singapore, a booking in our earlier years had us thinking that maybe our 'nice people' filter had failed us.

As the car pulled in beside the Barn and the family of four got out we approached them all smiles and welcomes expecting the first words to be about the beautiful alpacas they had been observing as they drove up the race. In fact the first words were about the alpacas.

Mrs. B, an elegantly and expensively dressed lady, gave us a tight smile of greeting and with a frown enquired, "Why have the alpacas all been shaved, you knew we were coming to see them?"

I could feel a shift in the force as Elaine's hackles began to rise in protest. My wife is an animal lover first and a tourism professional second and isn't one to back away from a confrontation.

There is no way in the world that we would have left the heavy fleeces on the alpacas in summer any longer than was absolutely necessary for anyone. Some of the larger animals carry an extra four to five kilo when fully fleeced and it needs to come off to avoid heat stress.

I quickly explained this to Mrs. B so hopefully we could move right along, watching Elaine glare at our guest as I did so.

Things appeared to have settled down as we showed them around the Barn, Mr. B and his young teenage daughters smiling away until Mrs. B returned from a look upstairs in the library/office/extra sofa divan accommodation room.

"Why are my husband and I not upstairs in the lovely room with the observation deck," she demanded, tight smile and questioning eyes once again in place.

Before I could reply Elaine took a step towards her and stated "because you booked in for a farm stay, we put you in the comfortable Barn Stay room with the cosy bed and ensuite rather than in the uncomfortable sofa divan bed in a room with no facilities."

Mr. B and I looked at each other and before Mrs. B could respond Elaine continued, "We have hosted many guests who have had a lovely time with us; however you do not appear comfortable about staying here so maybe its best if you just leave!"

The girls looked pleadingly at their mother who stood there open mouthed, her bluff having been called and her husband stared embarrassingly at his feet.

I thought we were all due for some 'time out' so I suggested that we would leave them for a few minutes to discuss what they would like to do and eased Elaine out of the door.

After about ten minutes during which time Elaine explained to me how she refused to be pushed around by any stuck up, well, you can imagine the rest, we returned to the Barn.

As we opened the door our guests approached us all genuine smiles with a much lighter atmosphere overhead and Mr. B explained it had been a long tiring day after many hours in the air, after an early start and they were here now and really happy to stay with us if that was still alright.

We said that was fine and then a very different Mrs. B asked Elaine if she had made the lovely garments, how nice they were and how clever she was.

Despite herself Elaine smiled and agreed that she had, and with the initial tension gone started showing her her creations.

The B family stayed with us for three days and had a ball. Mr. B was a jetliner pilot and a very interesting man and the girls really enjoyed the animals. Elaine offered to teach them how to spin and they enthusiastically agreed to give it a go.

It appeared that Mrs. B had quite a competitive personality and naturally assumed that she would be a better spinner than her daughters. To me, spinning is a little like the old rubbing your tummy and patting your head routine, easier for some than others but eventually with practice easy to do.

Elaine took great delight in watching an increasingly frustrated Mrs. B discover it was her daughters that were the naturals and not herself. The more Elaine had to stop and show Mrs. B once again the technique or repair her broken threads the more she and the daughters enjoyed it.

During their last day Mr. and Mrs. B asked us if we would like to join them for a bottle or two of red wine that evening as a thank you for their great stay.

Elaine and I could hardly believe it, what we had originally anticipated as our first guests from hell had been the very first ones to invite us for drinks with them; we happily accepted their offer and spent a most enjoyable and convivial couple of hours with them.

They left us the following day after hugs and kisses with a variety of homespun garments and a commission for Elaine to knit them a couple of alpaca beanies to post to them in Singapore.

As we waved them farewell we shook our heads in wonder at what an interesting world we lived in.

Another family from Asia, a middle aged couple travelling with their elderly parents also had an inauspicious start to their stay.

They had booked in for a couple of days in mid winter and unfortunately their dates had coincided with an unexpected snowfall that had lasted several days and rendered us completely white as far as the eye could see.

The afternoon they were to arrive we received a call from them explaining that they were travelling on a coach that was due to drop them off in Christchurch but the driver was happy to drop them off outside Warwickz Farm as they would be passing us and could we give the driver instructions.

This we duly did and I later waited on the other side of the highway in the lightly falling snow and sleet, rugged up as warm as I could get and looking like a yeti with my long winter snow flecked hair and beard.

Eventually, with numbing hands I watched the coach pull over to the shoulder of the highway throwing up a spray of icy muddy water over my boots, the uniformed driver bracing himself against the cold, quickly removed our guests luggage and left the five of us at the side of the highway surrounded by luggage as the snowfall began to increase its intensity.

I had a distinct feeling that the older couple had been peacefully sleeping in air conditioned comfort seconds before their arrival as they were looking very disoriented and confused. Where were they? Why were they now standing out in the snow and cold with not a sight of any civilization at all let alone some wonderful farm stay accommodation? Who was this hairy yeti like creature standing before them with a silly grin gesturing at some trees across the road?

It became immediately apparent that the older couple could not speak English so I then addressed the younger ones who fortunately spoke the lingo, explaining how it was too wet and snowy to drive our vehicle out to collect them and that they should follow me and they would be warm and sheltered in no time.

Some things are easier said then done. Trundling large cases through heavy snow and then waiting for a break in the traffic was just the beginning. The older guests were relieved though to notice a driveway through the gloom of the darkening afternoon and managed to get their second wind as our convoy slowly crunched our way across the paddocks of snow laden animals to the very inviting looking Red Barn.

Fortunately I had the foresight to have the heating on in the Barn so it was with much relief that they finally found sanctuary and I at last noticed some smiles as they settled in. I returned to the cottage to announce the successful arrival to Elaine thinking all my troubles were over when she asked.

"As they are not driving, what are the arrangements for their meals and are we supposed to drop them off somewhere or what?

"Shit", I replied heading towards the door and my wet coat and leaky boots.

While that was a very unpleasant winters day to arrive, we a year or so later, had a honeymooning couple from Singapore arrive on one of those glorious crisp sunny winter days. It was certainly cold but the sun was shining against the bluest of skies, it was one of those days that you felt great to be alive.

Our guests as you would imagine were absolutely buzzing on life, love and New Zealand and we all enjoyed a great afternoon visiting the animals and relating the stories. Warwickz Farm never looked better, all green grass and happy animals.

Elaine had made up the Barn Stay room with our Valentines Day theme, with the sexy red quilt and pillow cases, burgundy towels and so on. The bedside tables had heart shaped chocolates on them and a nice bottle of bubbly sat on a cushion of red rose petals in front of two crossed over champagne flutes. Breakfast was arranged for 8.00am the following morning.

Overnight, unbeknownst to neither our guests nor ourselves we had a huge amount of snow silently fall, so much snow that we were in white out conditions similar to the previous year. We were fortunate that while the snow had fallen in blizzard like quantities the weather had remained gorgeous, sunny, with blue skies.

As I approached the Barn with our guests all snuggled up in their love nest, curtained off to the rest of the world, I remembered how they had told me that this was their first time out of Singapore and smiled in anticipation of the surprise they were to shortly experience.

Everything except for the sides of the Barn and the very top of their rental cars red roof was blanketed in snow. It was white as far as the eye could see giving way to a bright blue sky on the horizon.

Knocking on the ranch slider door to their curtained room I stood there holding the breakfast tray, thick vapour coming from my grinning face as the groom with a returning smile drew the curtain and opened the door.

I watched in delight as his smile straightened out and his mouth formed a huge oval and his brown eyes continued to get wider and wider. I only wish I had had the foresight to have had my camera with me!

The whole world had changed overnight, a world that he had only seen in movies and pictures and I was delighted to have shared this experience with him.

Another, even more profound experience we were to enjoy was with a young teenaged boy from Japan who was staying with us for a week or so as part of an exchange visit with the local high school.

Young Tom had thoroughly enjoyed his time with us and made the most of the experience even to the extent of helping out with the not so popular farm chores. One evening though, towards the end of his stay he appeared to be lurking awkwardly about the kitchen window.

Asking him if anything was the matter he became a little embarrassed and said that everything was fine, though he continued to look a little anxious. When we gently asked him again he shyly asked me if I could take him outside and show him the stars.

I happily agreed and we went out along the driveway, away from the trees and looked up to the heavens. It was one of those nights when there wasn't a cloud in the sky and the night was lit up by one of the wonders of nature that most of us in our day to day lives fail to notice.

A million stars at least nestled on the black mantle of the sky in all their glory, every star sign represented in this majestic display. Tom explained that living all his 13 years in Tokyo, with its incandescent city light he had never really had the chance to properly look at the stars.

A lazy tear slipped down my cheek as I joined him in his state of wonder, feeling quite humble to share this exquisite and very personal moment with him.

Shona was a guest, originally from the Middle East, who had spent most of her working life in New York, in a challenging and successful career, more recently as a very senior executive of a powerful United

Nations organization and having recently retired was just beginning a well earned and long planned twelve months 'unofficial' travelling around the world.

Her three day visit in July coincided with three days of torrential rain which saw her marooned in the Barn. Having arrived by limousine, she was not able to drive to any indoor tourist venues that might have interested her and declined our offers to take her. She was thoroughly enchanted by her surroundings and our company.

We spent three days with her in the Barn, including sharing our meals together and we all had a wonderful time. Her vast experience of life at so many levels coupled with her intelligence and wisdom made her very stimulating company and she obviously enjoyed hearing about our experiences.

I absolutely hate it when our guests due to foul weather have little opportunity to get to see our menagerie close up and I was frequently scanning the dark clouds through the window hoping for a break in the weather.

The day of Shona's departure came all too soon, with the limousine booked to arrive late morning. I insisted that she be ready to depart an hour earlier than arranged so I could very slowly and with many stops take her on the farm tour by car.

She kept looking at Elaine in disbelief as I kept stopping the car and ducking out and coming back with a variety of chickens and rabbits and guinea pigs for her to hold and touch and enjoy as well as stopping beside the paddocks and parading pigs and goats and sheep and alpacas up to the fence line for her to view.

After three days in our company she already knew that she was in the company of an animal loony and settled back and enjoyed the farm safari.

She left us with warm memories of a special time and Elaine a commission to create an alpaca waistcoat similar to the one Shona had purchased for herself for her sister she would be meeting up with in Switzerland.

Shona went on to have a most amazing twelve month adventure, predominately around Asia which she shared with us in her private blog to friends and family. She would spend many weeks working with impoverished communities around the continent then spend some relaxation time in opulent resorts, then time with healers and monks enjoying every moment of it and making sure she supplied me with delicious descriptions of the gastronomic delights she was experiencing.

Our most mysterious hosting experience involved an older couple from Australia who arrived late one afternoon in early summer for a one night stay.

Arrangements had been made for me to return to them 30 minutes or so after they had settled in to take them on the 'tour'. However, as it was a Monday evening and bearing in mind that sometimes tours could go on for several hours, I suggested that it was probably wise for them to go out for their evening meal first and then enjoy the tour on their return, the summer evenings staying light until close to 10.00pm at that time of year.

They agreed that that was a splendid idea and could they pay for the room now rather than in the morning, which I happily agreed to, before returning to my late afternoon rounds of the animals.

A couple of hours later I was on standby for their return so we could start the tour before it got too late. Time ticked on with no sign of them and I was starting to become concerned an hour later with still no sign of them that they may have had a breakdown or perhaps worse.

I ventured over to the Barn and peered in at the room to discover that it was completely empty of any sign of our guests, including luggage. They had gone and the key had been left on the bed so they obviously had no intention of returning.

Oh well, I decided, that was easy money, no breakfasts, no room servicing and laundry to wash, a couple of extra hours free time, but I was still a little sad to think that they had got away without seeing all the animals.

Chapter Thirteen

Robbie & Rosie

Warwickz Farm is home to two of the most adorable Kunekune pigs whose offspring can be found right across New Zealand and Robbie is the most popular animal on the farm for many of our visitors.

Kunekune (pronounced kooney kooney) pigs are a New Zealand native pig. Unknown prior to the arrival of Europeans in New Zealand they are believed to have developed from pigs of Asian origin introduced approximately 200 years ago by whalers or traders.

Kept almost solely by Maori communities they were largely unknown to Europeans until the late 1970s when a joint excursion by Willowbank and Staglands Wildlife Reserves led to a small number of purebred Kunekunes being collected to form the basis of a captive breeding programme.

The descendents of these original 18 Kunekunes are now widely spread throughout New Zealand and some have been exported to the USA, UK and Europe.

The Polynesian word Kunekune simply means "plump plump" or "fat fat" and the fat content of the meat was used by pre European Maori communities to pack around food items in order to preserve them before they were buried underground.

Kunekune pigs are generally large fat animals that spend a lot of time just wallowing quietly in one place however Miniature Kunekunes' like Robbie and Rosie are much smaller and while still enjoying a good wallow are happy to leap into action on command and entertain and amuse you and your guests.

As mentioned in a previous chapter we take great delight in watching the reactions of our guests when we call the snoozing pigs over to say hi. They both leap into action and come bouncing across to the fence line in the hope of some food or a good scratch. Robbie can look a bit intimidating, especially to our younger visitors with his wild boar-like tusks but his big flat square face always appears to have a happy grin on it.

One of our very early bookings was a lovely older couple from New England in the States and the outgoing Beverley fell immediately in love with Robbie. After a couple of days I enquired of her slightly introverted husband George how he was enjoying himself and he confessed that everyday he was very hungry by lunch time. I asked if he would like us to give him a larger breakfast but he declined saying it would do no good as Beverley would still not let him eat any of his toast as she always collected it to feed to Robbie.

Another feature of the Kunekune that fascinates visitors is how hairy they are. They are not surprised when I relate to them that early last century it was not unusual to find paint brushes made from the bristles of Kunekunes.

Robbie and Rosie, whose aunty is on the front of the $2.00 NZ postage stamp featuring the Year of the Pig, happily graze on grass that provides most of what this intriguing breed requires for a healthy diet. This makes them much less prone to rooting up the ground looking for nutrition and making a muddy mess in the process. We supplement them with a daily bucket of soaked crushed barley mixed with cooked up vegetable scraps and in the colder months pig muesli or nuts that are specially formulated to maximize piggy health.

Rosie is such a wonderful mother; however we only breed her every two years as her fast growing piglets take a lot out of her and she is devoted to them. I was so proud to watch her once when her piglets were very young take a great deal of time and effort to organize herself so that when she fell on her side to feed them she wouldn't land on any of them. Ordinarily a normal pig would fall over whenever it was time and it was up to her young to make sure they were out of the way, survival of the fittest and smartest at work I suppose. I timed Rosie though and it took her nearly 2 minutes for her to finally lose her centre of balance and fall to the ground after ensuring all her piglets were finally safely out of the way.

Last season she surprised us by giving birth to eight piglets, Arlene, Charlene, Darlene, Karlene, Marlene, Fred, Ted and Jed, instead of her usual six.

We felt sorry for her in the weeks prior to birthing as she looked like she was dragging a set of bagpipes under her bulging belly. She gets very hot as she approaches her due date and we regularly shower her with buckets of water to cool her down, which she loves. Robbie however, if the slightest drop of water hits him goes off squealing in torment.

It is amazing how the number three occurs so often in the breeding of pigs. Every month Rosie has a three day window of opportunity to fall pregnant and when she does she is pregnant for 3 months, 3 weeks and 3 days. Fortunately she always has more than three piglets.

I remember her very first pregnancy, it was a beautiful sunny morning in mid spring and as soon as I finished my morning rounds I checked to see if there had been any developments overnight. I could hear soft grunting coming from Rosie's little wooden house as I approached and looking inside found Rosie laying on her side looking absolutely exhausted with six little creatures snuggled up against her belly in a heap.

It really was an enchanting scene, the piglets would have been born in the early hours as they were all warm and dry, they were so tiny and oh so cute. There was a creamy coloured one, a ginger one and two black and white spotted ones and two ginger and black spotted ones, all fast asleep.

Not able to help myself I reached in and stroked the spotted one on top of the heap, his short bristles and wrinkly skin toasty to the touch. It squirmed slightly under my fingers and emitted a soft squeaky grunt. This started a chain reaction as the one below him also squirmed and opened its eyes and within a second the whole heap came to life and eagerly attached themselves to the nearest of Rosie's nipples for breakfast.

Rosie looked up at me with an expression that seemed to ask me, why did I have to do that. She looked totally spent, it had been a long night for her and I did feel a little guilty about waking up the little treasures. I stroked her face and back as she lay on her side letting the little ones ravish her, after a while I was starting to feel part of the family.

A short while later they finished their slurping and Rosie decided she needed to change her position for a more comfortable one and slowly and carefully repositioned herself looking even more tired than before. Her little darlings went back to pushing and shoving against her though this time not looking for food. I felt so sorry for her, all she wanted to do was sleep and recover a little from her ordeal.

I decided that having interrupted her sleeping earlier I should now make amends, so I eased myself deeper into her house and laying on my side gently eased the piglets over to lay against me for a while to give Rosie a well deserved breather. It was an experience I will never forget that still brings a huge smile to my face whenever I remember it. These six beautiful new born, tiny, gorgeous piglets with their intoxicating new life scent to them were all snuggled up against my shirt and all fast falling asleep. I looked across at Rosie who was snoring loudly and knew she was aware that her new borns were in safe hands and so could rest peacefully for a while.

The warm sunshine was beaming in on us and the rich depth of colours, nestled against me, were illuminated in all their glory. I could feel the warmth and the rhythm of the breathing of the piglets, each as big as my hand, through my shirt. I do not think I have ever felt more content and at peace as I did just laying their with my temporarily adopted porcine family. I was not aware that I too had drifted off to sleep with them until Elaine, who had been wondering what had happened to me eventually, saw my foot protruding through the entrance to Rosie's house and gave it a gentle nudge.

Smiling down at me, she shook her head and with a sigh said "Chris, you know it's the mother that needs to bond with her young, not the farmer."

"She has," I replied, "and so now have I"

Each of Robbie and Rosie's piglets has found wonderful homes over the years all around the country. We ask top dollar for them to ensure their now owners value them and they leave us with a kit that includes their registration papers, vet check paperwork, weaner pellets, a piglet health food supplement and an information pack on the breed and general health advice.

Anyone taking a piglet also has on-going access to us for any advice they may require in the future. We also give them a briefing of the basic dos and don'ts and things we have learnt over time. One important instance of this is the fact that as pigs do not have a gag reflex, if they are given a large round piece of apple or carrot or whole slice of bread they can very easily choke, therefore it is important to give them bite size portions. We do not let our piglets go to just anyone and in this way have ensured that the right people with the appropriate accommodations have them and have made some good friends in the process.

One very young couple who took a piglet many years ago became regular visitors to Warwickz Farm. Their piglet who they named Professor Spots spent his nights nice and warm in the laundry room of their house and had a large basket in the back of their station wagon for travelling around in. They were concerned that he may be missing his parents and they missing him so for a while they brought him back to say hi.

I cannot say whether either piggy party was overjoyed at the reunion, but we were. It was wonderful to see one our babies back for a visit and watch the various stages of his growth. Kunekunes are highly intelligent, up there with the most intelligent of dogs, and Pro Spots enjoyed showing off his new skills. He had been trained to walk on a harness and could go fetch and beg for food.

One day we received a call from the Rare Breeds Conservation Society of Canterbury, of which we are members, asking if we could take Robbie or Rosie to an upcoming Pet Expo where the Society was running a stand. Unfortunately neither of them is trained to walk and so are not travel friendly so we contacted Pro Spots owners and they were only too happy to oblige.

Elaine and I decided to visit the Expo and eventually we came across the Rare Breeds section. One enclosure in particular was raising a lot of interest and on closer inspection, well as close as we could get at the edge of the crowd, we noticed it was Professor Spots who was entertaining the crowd. We were delighted and called out 'well done' Professor Spots and we were very surprised, as were his fans, at his reaction. He had recognised our voices and interrupted his act to go to the corner of the crowd where we were to say hi.

We would not have believed that after 9 months away from us he would still not only recognise us but also want to greet us. We felt quite humble and very proud as we waved him goodbye and left him to his bemused fans.

The arrival of our Kunekune piglets is a real highlight of the years we have them and while the joy of living and working with these little characters is wonderful, they can be quite mischievous at times as they get older.

The very first time we heard an alpaca honk was due to the piglets. Alpacas as well as being gentle creatures are also very quiet animals and if you hear any sound from them it is usually the gentle soft humming sound of contentment. So, it was with some concern that I looked around trying to locate the source of this frantic honk honk honk honking.

I traced the honks to Hotsocks one of our older wethers who is the guardian alpaca of the herd and always alert for any potential danger. He was alerting the rest of the herd to this never seen before procession of freshly escaped highly mobile, very small, colourful bristly creatures heading their way at speed.

Elaine trains the piglets to beg for food with pieces of apple that she holds above their heads and it is not long before they are polished beggars, rearing up on their hind legs in a cute pleading gesture, and also juicy apple lovers. Elaine last season came in from giving the piglets their very first taste of apple and was just starting to tell me about how much they enjoyed it when we heard the thunka thunka thunka thunka of three sets of tiny trotters bounding up the hallway and into the kitchen looking for more pieces of apple.

As the piglets get older they begin to range further afield but always appear to stay within sight of Rosie, albeit at times several hundred metres away. With a brisk shake of the weaner pellet bucket though they come racing back to Rosie's paddock often from a number of directions. For the piglets, like me, the allure of a good feed is always great incentive to return to base.

By the time they are ready to leave us, if they can still squeeze under the fences, they no longer wait for us to feed them but come and actively seek us out. If they are not successful in their mission they will then venture into the garage and attempt to pilfer any unsecured apples from the crates along with anything else that could be potentially tasty, all the while grunting in anticipation.

Life slowly returns to normal as we wave a fond farewell to the last piglet and it probably takes a good few weeks to get used to these real characters not being here. We usually spend a bit of quality time with Robbie and Rosie as we recall with a smile the numerous incidents we enjoyed, memories that will stay with us forever.

Chapter Fourteen

Steering and Shearing

The stock truck slowly beep beep beeped its way up Poultry Lane to the gate where we had the stock loading ramp, we had borrowed, waiting for it to be hooked onto the back of the truck. As he got closer to us the smiling face of the burly truckie noticed the temporarily rigged up electric fencing and the two black steers standing grazing nearby.

His smile gave way to a frown as he slowly shook his head and stated that he would give it 30 minutes and then he would have to be off.

"No worries," I replied, "we will have them up the ramp in a minute and you're away."

A resigned knowing smile returned to his face as he looked at his watch but he remained silent, though I could certainly read his mind, 'bloody lifestylers' he was thinking.

183

Eighteen months or so earlier a friend had asked if we would like to buy a couple of his freshly weaned Angus steer calves, suggesting that we could sell one to the works to pay for the butchery of the other one to keep us in tender steaks and roasts for the duration.

This was while I was still in 'paid' employment and before the Barn was built and the extra fencing put in. What a delicious idea I thought as I began selling the idea to Elaine trying not to salivate too much.

It had involved a bit more work than I had anticipated over the period as they transformed from cute calves to large unnamed black beasts. Having large open paddocks in those days we had to use electric fencing to allow them to strip graze and that meant having to constantly supply fresh water to their temporary troughs, as well as regularly move the fencing.

When the snows came there was even more work feeding out hay and rounding them up and returning them when the heavily snow laden fencing collapsed or the power went out and they found they were free. What kept me going though in the rougher weather was the thought of char grilled steak with Elaine's wild plum sauce.

The day though had arrived and we went to usher the black monsters into the truck. Walking behind the first one we got him with gentle encouragement from a large stick just about to the base of the ramp. He decided that there was soon to be nowhere else to go except up, and he didn't do up, so he decided to take a detour through the electric fencing.

Knowing that the steers were used to staying within the confines of the fencing we had decided not to heat it, not expecting them to take detours through it. We rounded him up for another go and put the fencing back in place and to the amusement of the driver repeated the process. They reckon the definition of insanity is repeating the same thing over and over again and expecting a different result. Well, I must shamefully admit that we were classically insane that morning and only had a rethink when the driver gave us our 5 minute warning.

By this time I had reinforced the electric with some lengths of timber and various other barriers and we decided to try to stampede both steers up the ramp. The truckie by now was thoroughly enjoying the entertainment and really started to giggle as he watched us with blood curdling cries charge towards the beasts and force them into serious movement. They ran towards the single ramp neck to neck not having time to look for a suitable spot to detour through due to screaming banshees that were assailing them. Before they knew it they were at the ramp and as one peeled off to crash through the barrier the other one hurtled upwards and onto the truck.

The driver appeared quite impressed and was still chuckling to himself as he headed off to the works with a promise to return the following day and no doubt looking forward to sharing his amusing mornings experience with the boys back at the depot over a few beers. Latching the gate behind him we went off to see where the other steer had got to.

Not wanting to endure a repeat of the mornings performance, especially in front of an audience, the driver would probably be selling tickets by now, we had a total rethink.

We decided that while the sheep yards were far too small height wise for cattle, with a little creativity I could convert the one opening onto the lane, to accommodate our steers, and then run them from it, up the ramp and onto the truck. We decided to wait until Bruce returned from work to give us a hand with the now single steer and I set about building the fortress.

Later that afternoon the cow folk were back on the prairie trying to round up the herd of one. He was now very wary and pretty nervous now that his brother had left him and very skittery. On our numerous approaches he easily managed to break away further into the open paddock away from the gate. We had a new audience, the ever watchful alpacas watching in wonder from a neighbouring paddock.

Doubled over, trying to regain our breath after another abortive attempt to run him in the direction of the gate we decided it was time to deploy the truck. The idea was that Elaine would drive the old Toyota Hilux and try to trap him in a corner of the paddock while I sat in the passenger seat with a lassoed rope, trying to lasso him through the open door as he ran or when trapped leap out and attach the rope over his head to we could lead him.

It is obvious to me now that throwing a lassoed rope from a moving vehicle over the head of a moving animal is something that requires not just good skills but also a lot of practice, neither of which I possessed. Suffice to say that we were only left with the alternative of trapping him somewhere.

On three occasions Elaine who by now was thoroughly enjoying the boy racing experience of bouncing across the paddock, throwing the wheel aggressively from extreme left to extreme right and coming to whiplash inducing emergency stops, had had him cornered. On each occasion I had leapt out only to have him find a second wind and crash through the undergrowth or under a tree and twice leaving large dents on the mudguards make his escape.

We really thought we had him though when Elaine had him caught between the Toyota and a huge gorse bush. I attempted to open my door fully so I could get out only to find I was also trapped between the the vehicle and the gorse bush and not willing to climb through it Elaine had to reluctantly reverse, calling me a chicken and set him free again.

The next manoeuvre unfortunately brought us a whole new set of problems. Running him along the macrocarpa hedge along the side of Mr. Thompson's farm and with Elaine swerving in to trap him, the steer dived under the hedge and managed to bounce himself over the short sheep fence and onto Mr. Ts place, ooops.

Bruce and I then spent the next hour or so furtively stalking our prey across someone else's farm, Elaine I think went to hide inside. We managed to keep him as close to the Warwickz Farm boundary as possible with the aid of a couple of six metre lengths of pvc piping we carried as arm extensions.

It was fine getting him close to home but how do you get a steer across a boundary without a gate we asked ourselves between puffs. We decided that if he could go one way there was no reason why he couldn't go the other way, memories of his brother's rush up the ramp coming back to me.

Locating a shorter section of fence line, very close to where Harry the Gotland sheep pushed under several years later, Bruce and I forming a flying V shape gathered what was left of our remaining breath and with loud howls charged at him. He raced towards the fence and managed to straddle it breaking a post in half in the process but did manage to bounce back onto the Warwickz Farm side.

He was now in the paddock with the alpacas, which while now on home soil was not a good place for him to be. Marshalling the last of our resources we repeated our successful charge and managed to get the steer to repeat his response as he charged through the fence back to the paddock where we had all stared from 3 hours earlier, once again breaking a fencepost in the process.

Taking a few paces away from the fence line the steer crashed to the ground in an exhausted heap and so did we, totally spent.

That evening we cancelled the stock truck and arranged for the home kill guy to come round and take care of our quarry first thing in the morning. When he arrived the steer was still resting where he had fallen and didn't know a thing as he was dispatched by his unseen assassin, his tender meat all now rested and unstressed. The butcher promising to have our tasty meat cuts ready in a few days, left us the steers tail to be getting on with.

I am pretty sure it was a psychological thing going back to caveman days when the hunter returned home with the kill that he had been stalking for days, but I swear that that ox tail stew we enjoyed that evening was the most mouth watering, tastiest piece of meat that I have ever enjoyed.

There are two major shearing events, well major, in terms of a smallholding I suppose, at Warwickz Farm, which is when we shear the alpacas in November and then the sheep closer to Christmas.

Shearing alpacas is quite a different job to shearing sheep, it is a bit more specialised and the animals are larger and more valuable so more care is needed with them. We can take off close to 5 kilograms of fibre from our larger alpacas like River and Shyloh which is why it is important to get the fleece off them as early as possible in summer once the A & P Shows are over.

The large stud boys can be appear quite intimidating when handling them when fully fleeced, especially when walking them past the girls who they want to party with or the other boys who they want to impress with their dominance. You have to have your wits about you as you guide them into the shearing yards. It always makes me smile though after they have been freshly shorn when I return them to their paddocks wondering what I was worried about with this skinny goat like thing I am leading.

Our alpacas are shorn lying on the ground stretched out and restrained by ropes at their feet. This way they feel safe and secure, at half time we change sides and shear the other side and then they are released to get up and enjoy their feeling of lightness. The only alpacas who ever take exception to such indignities occasionally are the studs. If anyone is going to squeal and wet themselves you can guarantee it is going to be a boy.

I sound as if I am a seasoned shearer when I am in fact a seasoned shearer's gofer and general roustabout. We employ the services of a delightful couple Ron and Kathy to shear our alpacas. Ron has lived many lives including being a sheep shearer for many years and for the last decade or so an alpaca shearer.

Ron, in his late 60s is as thin as a rail and as fit as a fiddle, a real country gentleman always ready to greet you with his huge grin. Kathy, his long suffering wife whom he carts around the South Island along with his shearing and camping gear sits on the alpacas as he shears and gives them a pedicure and checks their teeth and berates Ron for any slivers of fibre that he misses.

Ron and Kath, who live on a small farm in the breathtaking Caitlins region of Otago are in semi retirement but have for many years now combined their shearing business with music. Ron is a well regarded country and western singer who regularly entertains at the Golden Guitar Country Music Festival in Tamworth in Australia and other events in New Zealand.

We, as often as possible conclude a long days shearing with Ron and Kath staying in the Barn and Ron serenading us with his guitar and repertoire of original and popular songs after a well earned barbeque and a few cold beers.

Getting the alpacas to and from the shearing yards using the raceway has made life a lot easier over the years, we run them down in groups into separate yards, all the girls together, the wethers together and the youngsters with their Mums. The studs we bring through after all the others have been shorn so save any nonsense.

Our clever alpacas have learnt to put themselves back where they belong. Once shorn they are released back into the raceway system where they wait for their buddies and then slowly wander back to where they have come from. We then simply close the gate behind them once the next yards worth of alpacas are ready to be shorn.

If only it was that easy with the sheep. The smaller flock isn't too bad with Nova and her family and the Gotlands using the race to get to the yards. It is the larger flock of 30 odd black and coloured sheep and arapawas and their crosses that we have the fun with. They are in the large 5 acre paddock on the southern part of Warwickz Farm with the nursery/duck paddock between them and Poultry Lane, part of the race system.

Part one of the exercise entails rounding up the sheep and getting them into the nursery paddock. I must look a sight racing around the paddock on my old bike trying to keep the herd in a block that tends to leak at both ends and run them through a small gate in a very large paddock.

There is always one who wants to break away in the opposite direction and bring a couple of mates with him. Part one successfully accomplished, we move on to the more challenging stage two and that is getting them out of the nursery paddock and into the Lane through a very small gate that only opens 45 degrees.

The gate is in the middle of the huge macrocarpa hedge halfway along the paddock, barely recognisable in the shadows of the hedge. The trick I have learnt over the years is to partition off the half of the paddock to the east of the gate and try to build a chute for the sheep to follow down and then through the gate.

As the sheep enter the nursery paddock they slow down to gaze upon the surreal mess I have made of the paddock. They are confronted by a barrier made up of a short reel of wire net fencing attached to a ride-on mower trailer, a large rusted out wheelbarrow, some handmade wooden gates and a couple of lengths of plastic piping. Alongside this monstrosity on the other side of the gate is a similar collection of paddock debris hoping to entice the sheep to funnel through the gate.

It used to be a nightmare trying to stampede them through such a small opening and inevitably they would get stressed and as they got to the far end of the paddock the arapawas and arapawa crosses would bounce over the fence and we would be back to square one.

Now it is just a matter of slowly but steadily running them along the newly sculptured paddock barrier and gently through the gate and into Poultry Lane which has been likewise barricaded to stop them running in the wrong direction or behind the chook houses. It is then only a short distance to the yards.

There is always at least one sheep that loses the plot completely as we finally approach the yards, and decides to circle back and try to retrace its reluctant steps back to where it came from. Hopefully I can catch it before it leaps over any barrier, which then needs to be broken down so it can return, and manhandle it to the yards. A large wooly beastie that does not want to cooperate can put a bit of a strain on an aging body and I am ready for a bit of a break before the shearer arrives.

As the shearer works his way through the two flocks, Elaine sweeps up the mess before Bruce and I manhandle another one onto the shearing mat and then we slowly but steadily fill the woolsacks, skirting the daggy edges of the fleeces as we go.

Once the sheep is shorn we all stand back as it leaps to its feet feeling much lighter and a bit disoriented and charges around looking for the exit which it duly finds and joins the other skinny creatures in the lane.

Recently we have begun using another shearer who is much better set up than the previous one. His 4WD vehicle tows a trailer with what looks like a stage set up on it and he parks it in the paddock alongside the yards.

Using some mobile gates he runs half a dozen sheep at a time into a holding pen next to the shearing 'stage' and then pulls one through the one-way swing doors, shears it and then eases it off the back of the stage in one seamless motion. We collect the wool and quickly run the broom across the stage and it is on to the next one.

We now find the shearing is done in half the time and I am not afterwards groaning and complaining of sore muscles, it also means it only takes two of us to assist as well.

Once the shearing is over and we gaze in wonder at the skinny, bright looking sheep with their variety of spots and colours and then they easily and happily return to their respective paddocks in an orderly fashion. After a tidy up and the collection and storage of the fully laden wool sacks we head for the cottage for a cold beer and a wine for Elaine and some nice roast lamb for dinner.

Chapter Fifteen

Special Friends

It has been a privilege over the years to have spent time with such a variety of creatures that have been real characters and that have bonded with so well. One of them is Nova whose story starts even before she was born.

The earth crunched under my feet as I made my way across the ice encrusted paddocks, pulling my beanie tighter over my blue tipped ears. The first serious frost of the season had dawned on this crisp, sunny but very cold morning in late August.

On my return route to our warm cottage after releasing the ducks and pigeons from their overnight accommodations and having fed the rabbits their morning breakfast of hay I glanced into the house paddock to see how our heavily pregnant goats were faring on this chilly morning.

It was then that I noticed the small white bundle of dreadlocks lying still, next to Rags, one of our angora does. My worst fears were confirmed on gently lifting the cold yet perfectly formed angora kid whose eyes while lifeless seemed to project a certain serenity as if triumphant that it had at last completed its journey into life, albeit a short and cold one.

Rags did not appear to be overly concerned at her loss but I thought it might be wise to release some of the pressure off her bulging udder, which I gently did, releasing the frothy hot colostrum into an enamel bowl.

Three months later it is early November, the sun was shining warmly and the paddocks are alive with fast maturing frolicking lambs and kids. It is with some surprise therefore when Elaine appears in the doorway holding a new born lamb in her arms still half encased in its birth sac, a gorgeous arapawa-romney cross ewe lamb obviously abandoned by its mother minutes after birth.

A number of thoughts race through our minds; surprise at the discovery, sadness at the abandonment, horror at the thought that this new creature will perish as she had not tasted her mothers life sustaining colostrum and then great relief that the little angora kids lost life would not now be in vain.

Nova the lamb is now a six year old great, great, grandmother who believes she is as much human as sheep. Rag's Colostrum gave her the essential kick-start to life that allowed us to bottle feed her and she is now a popular attraction for visitors to Warwickz Farm.

Featuring prominently in the animal encounter events we stage for young people Nova is not only of educational interest, she also allows us to remember and recall that precious little bundle of dreadlocks born one freezing cold August morning.

Our larger than life Buff Orpington rooster, Bartie, who unfortunately past away this last summer, became a Warwickz Farm star attraction over the years. Buff Orpingtons are a very large chicken, especially the roosters; they have a beautiful golden colour and are one of the gentlest breeds of large fowl.

A friend of ours was looking to find a good home for the middle aged Bartie and as he was such a commanding looking guy who would definitely enhance Polutry Lane we took him on, little knowing what an asset he was to become in so many ways.

Never having really been handled before, this large guy was initially reluctant to be picked up but it wasn't long before he was letting me cradle him like a baby as we sat down for a chat about life on Poultry Lane.

He settled in fairly easily, though it took a good few weeks for the pecking order among the other free ranging roosters to bed in, many of them wanted to prove themselves against the new, big guy. Bartie was basically a pacifist who could hold his own in a scrap but would rather walk or in many cases run away then face a confrontation.

We decided that he deserved his own night time quarters where he wouldn't be troubled by any would-be cock of the walk young roosters and so we set him up in his apartment at the end of Poultry Lane where he would spend his nights, before free ranging, or in his later years lounging behind the chook houses, during the day.

Feeding time on Poultry Lane is always chaotic with dozens of free ranging chooks, ducks, geese, turkeys and guinea fowl getting in the way as the purebreds in their coops are feed, each fighting for their share of any dropped feed.

Bartie and I had a system whereby he would join the waiting throng as I opened the gate and once I had my bucket ready I would steadily head for his quarters while he ran ahead of me. Halfway along Poultry Lane the throng would be keeping up with us and would start jostling each other for position. That was when Bartie with a nifty side step would take a detour around the back of the chook houses where there was no traffic and race me to our rendezvous.

I would inevitably get there seconds before him allowing me time to open the door, reach down to him as he arrived from the far side of the coop and scoop him up and inside and then fill his food bowl and freshen up his water all to the disgust and dismay of the other free rangers at this special treatment.

Bartie who decided he quite enjoyed being cradled in my arms like a big feathery golden baby, and I used to enjoy our frequent chats. If I had been working somewhere close by for a period and felt like a short break Bartie was only too happy to climb aboard for a cuddle.

I used to marvel at the size of his feet with their long talons and his thick scaly legs; you could definitely understand how chickens were descended from dinosaurs. I used to massage the soles of his feet with their fatty pads that felt and looked pretty much like plump pockets of human flesh, warm and soft to the touch. With my hand pushing against his foot he would spread out his talons and they would cover three quarters of my hand.

One late afternoon we were awaiting the arrival of some overseas guests and Bartie and I were sitting on the little bench seat at the entrance to the driveway ready to welcome them to Warwickz Farm. It had been a lovely warm sunny day and we were enjoying our peaceful sojourn as late afternoon turned into early evening and I noticed that Bartie whose feet I had been massaging had fallen sound asleep.

It is quite a humbling experience to realise that a non domestic animal that is laying on its back which, being an extremely vulnerable position would go against all natural instincts of survival, trusts you to the extent that they would go to sleep in that position. It was a very deep sleep and unless I had heard it with my own ears I would not have believed it, he was actually snoring very lightly. I spent the remaining time until the guests arrived sitting there with a huge grin on my face.

It became a regular thing during our times together that I would press Barties feet against my hand so they would splay out and it wasn't long before this ritual evolved into his sitting upright in my arms giving high fives to anyone who wanted one.

Over his time Bartie would have given close to a thousand high fives. I arranged a seat for us to sit next to his apartment where he could entertain his fans. It was a regular feature during the warmer months for primary school children and pre school groups to surround us, a sea of smiling and sometimes slightly nervous young faces tentatively putting their hands out for a high 5 and then backing up for a second one.

The looks of sheer joy at the experience on some of the faces and the huge wide eyed wonder at what was happening still makes me smile today. I found that what was especially satisfying was watching some of the more timid children overcome their fears and witnessing their bravery being rewarded by the happiness radiating from their faces.

After everyone had had their high 5s Bartie would do his party trick for them, and that was by playing 'dead rooster'.

I would pick up Bartie, place him on his back and slide him onto my outstretched hand, balancing him and supporting his back. He would then in a very short time nod off to sleep. As he lost consciousness his feet would relax and hang down and his head would flop to the side and also hang down so much so that you would swear that he was a dead rooster. I would then walk around as if I was a waiter carrying a tray of feathery rooster.

Returning him to an upright position he would slowly wake up and then I would put him in his sitting upright position and he would wave (with a little help from) his huge foot in goodbye to his new friends as they went on with Elaine to continue their tour.

The 'dead rooster' routine came back to haunt me in the last three weeks of Barties life. On three separate occasions I went in the morning to help the now arthritic Bartie from his apartment only to find him lying on his back, his legs in the air and his head hanging down on one side. Wiping away a tear, I went to remove his body when he suddenly started shaking himself awake much to my delight.

He had found this very vulnerable position so comfortable he had rolled over onto his back and due to his size and arthritis could not turn back over, three times the old fellow had me going.

I am pleased to report that it wasn't a matter of finding the deceased Bartie alone and cold in his coop one morning. In his later years he had had a stroke and he was having trouble keeping his balance and he had started to lose a bit of weight, we therefore knew he didn't have much longer with us.

One sunny Saturday morning over the Christmas break I let him out of his coop and I sensed it was going to be his last day. We set him up in a very comfortable crate with some soft straw and food and water and brought him up to the cottage where he spent his last morning enjoying the warm sunshine in the courtyard, surrounded by people who loved him before quietly and peacefully slipping away. We couldn't ask for a more perfect way for our dearly beloved Bartie to leave us. I am sure the angels are getting a buzz out of their newly arrived high fiving friend.

Another special friend is Sassy, she is a buff coloured Chinese silkie chicken, although we are sure that she doesn't really think she is a chicken.

Sassy was hatched out of an incubator and after the requisite time under the heat lamps keeping her toasty warm as she grew into a strong fluffy chicken we attempted to introduce her to another chinese silkie hen to bring her up.

Chinese silkies are a wonderful bantam (small sized) breed of chicken that are relatively rare and are famous for their very silky and fluffy appearance. They have black skin and an extra toe to other breeds and a bright blue ear lobe. They are also famous for being one of the broodiest breeds of chicken and are happy to hatch out and bring up any other breed of chicken and more as in Sassy's case.

However, when we tried to introduce Sassy to her step mother she took great exception and insisted we take her out of this strange feathery place and bring her back home and she wanted a coffee to steady her nerves. Well, maybe not the coffee, but she certainly didn't want to have anything to do with the big feathery thing.

It wasn't long before she was living in her own purpose built apartment near the Enderby Island rabbits. Meanwhile she had proved quite friendly and before long I had her sitting up like a human in my hand and riding along on my shoulder like a pirate's parrot.

It was not long after, that Sassy became a stop on the tour, some light relief after learning all about the Enderbys and their story of evolution. There must be countless photos of Sassy, all around the world sitting on a delighted tourists head and posing for the camera.

Sometimes, particularly with tours of youngsters, Sassy will sit on my shoulder as I meet and greet them and come along on the tour with us. Inevitably I will need to take her off my shoulder so I can attend to some other animal encounter and she will quite happily stay where I place her for as long as it takes, usually on top of something, where she is nice and safe. I have to confess though that on a few occasions, many hours after our visitors have left us or our guests have returned to the Barn I have notice that Sassy is not about and hastily return to where I left her, where she is still patiently waiting for my return. I have given her an extra treat on those occasions to try to salve my guilt.

Generally Sassy free ranges all day and is put to bed at night. She spends her time around the cottage and gardens and never ventures down to Poultry Lane where those buck bucking feathery things live. We had become used to recognising Sassy as Sassy, rather than a chicken, so we were slightly surprised one day to find an egg sitting in her bedroom one morning, followed by five more over the next week. After the sixth one was laid Sassy decided to sit on them.

Sassy, not being a chicken, had never been anywhere near a rooster so we knew she was on a hiding to nothing sitting on her eggs. Elaine selected some fertile eggs laid by other bantam hens and we discreetly made the switch. Twenty one days later a very proud Sassy hatched out five fluffy balls of joy. We had found ourselves the perfect incubator.

Over the years Sassy has hatched dozens of eggs and has brought up the chicks to a healthy and happy maturity. Suffice to say we have a few more chooks living around the cottage now.

Faced with a dilemma one day when a guinea fowl who had been sitting on the communal nest decided to desert her post about 5 days before they were due to hatch, we turned to Sassy for assistance. She was more than happy to confine herself to her apartment for the period and duly hatched out most of the eggs.

As the weeks turned into months Sassy continued to dote over her charges as they grew into a strong healthy mix of lavender and pearl guinea fowl that inevitably outgrew her both literally and emotionally.

They used to follow her around all day pecking around the gardens and lawns and then all line up as she led them up the ramp to the increasingly crowded bedchamber at night. They all slowly in ones and twos joined up with the free ranging flock of guinea fowl who have been patrolling Warwickz Farm for many years now.

A couple of years ago one of the guinea fowls hatched nine keats (guinea fowl chicks) and being a hopeless mother decided she had done her bit and after a few hours left them to fend for themselves.

Fortunately we had been monitoring the nest and it wasn't long before we became aware of the situation and managed to catch the cute stripy little things. Guinea fowl are notoriously hard to raise, particularly in the colder months, originally from West Africa, cold Canterbury days are not conducive to optimal keat health.

Having collected them all we were at a bit of a loss to know what to do with them until Elaine decided that Sassy might be able to save the day. Sure enough, she adopted the little ones and as she had previously, happily and proudly brought them up to full maturity.

With Sassy's high workload we thought it was only fair to ease her burden a little and so I started training Cybil, a white chinese silkie, who showed similar potential to Sassy.

When Sassy is busy sitting or looking after chickies, Cybil is happy to do the 'parrot' thing on my shoulder and the 'head' thing with the tourists. Cybil free rangers full time and never really took to the idea of being put away nice and safe and secure at night in her chalet alongside the cottage.

Elaine used to enjoy watching me through the kitchen window trying to grab Cybil to put her away at night. She would happily let me pick her up during the day, but in the evenings she would give me a major runaround, ducking and diving and playing peek-a-boo from the other side of trees or beneath hard to reach places.

She is certainly bright though and realised that if I gave up completely and left her to it and went inside she would miss out on her tea. This scenario more times than not ensued and she would immediately relinquish the chase and come up to me as I approached the cottage and crouch down for me to pick her up, put her to bed but most importantly, feed her. Something I could really relate to.

Chapter Sixteen

Decent Exposure

As the years go by and we live the lifestyle along with its ups and downs and challenges and joys, we may not enjoy much in the way of prosperity or leisure time but the time we have is quality time, surrounded by the things we love.

Concentrating on what we do at Warwickz Farm we often do not notice how far we have come and it is the occasional wake up from the outside world that gives us a bit of perspective.

An example of this is the increasing number of phone calls and emails we receive, generally two or three a week from people seeking either our advice on the care of, or problems with, their animals or wanting to purchase some of ours. Google being an everyday part of people's worlds it is not long before we are found either through our site or on other listings, especially the Rare Breeds Conservation Society website.

At first this was rather daunting; who did people think we were, to come to us for advice, a redundant businessman and a retired nurse. It was only after speaking to these callers at length about the given subject that we realised just how much knowledge we had gained through sheer experience backed up with our own research to attend to our own needs.

Some of the assistance Elaine has given has been on-going resulting in immense satisfaction. A recent case in point was the increasing concern of an older lady owner of a very pregnant miniature Kunekune sow crossed with a full sized kunekune pig, who appeared to be overdue. She had never owned pigs before and was besotted with them and anguished about making sure all would be well with the birthing.

Over the course of a few weeks there were numerous conversations of various lengths about the matter and eight piglets were duly born to Elaine's and the owners delight. However that was not the end of the matter, a further few weeks worth of conversation regarding the runt of the litter ensued. The little fellow was just not growing although it did appear that he was getting his share of his mother's bounty. The inevitable death of the little thing due to a birth defect was anticipated by Elaine who eased the owner into her upcoming grief with care and sensitivity, her nursing experience coming into play.

A few months later her and her husband made the long trip up to Warwickz Farm to meet us and put a face to that lovely lady I am proud to call my wife and thank her so much for her help. They were also delighted to see what purebred miniature Kunekunes were like when we all spent some quality time with Robbie and Rosie.

Other enquiries we have had have led to us meeting up with a variety of owners of chickens and sheep and goats to name a few. Elaine has become our resident unpaid animal consultant on the farm.

It was very gratifying one day when Elaine answered a call for assistance from Te Papa, the National Museum of New Zealand in Wellington.

Preparing for their upcoming Kahu Ora/Living Cloaks education program showcasing the world's largest collection of Maori cloaks they had come across a mystery. The cloaks are regarded as living cloaks and carry powerful stories of their weavers and wearers, a continuing link between Maori ancestors and descendents, so it was important that everything was done correctly. A very unusual fibre had been found in one of the ancient cloaks and they needed to discover what it was and they wanted to scientifically compare it with pure angora/mohair fibre to see if it was of wooly goat origin.

We were only too happy to oblige and sent off a sample for them to examine. Te Papa came back to us thanking us for our assistance and sending some information on the exhibition and confirming that they had now solved the mystery and it had indeed come from an angora goat which not being native to New Zealand must have quietly sneaked into the country many many years ago. Hanging up the telephone we felt very proud to be consultants to the National Museum of New Zealand.

One afternoon we received a phone call from Keith Stewart who at the time hosted the Saturday evening prime time slot on a national radio station, a show celebrating food and wine. He was doing some research for a feature on where our finer food comes from before it reaches the chefs kitchen.

I was able to give him a run down on our three varieties of rare breed ducks, all of whose bodies are too heavy for them to fly. One thing led to another and we spent an enjoyable time discussing Warwickz Farm creatures.

So enjoyable was the time that before he hung up he asked me if I wouldn't mind being a part of his show in a couple of weeks time for about 5 to 10 minutes so he could interview me and I could repeat some of my stories.

The night duly arrived and I was onto my third glass of red by 8.30pm feeling a little nervous about addressing the whole nation when his producer rang to put me on standby. Not wanting to be distracted by the family laughing at me I took the phone into the bedroom and anxiously waited, watching myself in the wall to ceiling closet door mirrors nervously gulping at my wine glass.

I do not presume in any way to be an entertainer, but the 5 to 10 minutes turned into close to 30 minutes as I watched myself in the mirror, arms gesticulating dramatically as I waxed lyrical about our feathered creatures and the antics they get up to. A still chuckling Keith Stewart thanked me very much as the program broke for the news and I hurriedly got in a plug for our website and returned, buzzing, to the lounge room and the applause of the family.

Twelve months later we received a call from the host of a popular country life program on Radio National who asked if he and a soundman could come and spend some time with me walking along Poultry Lane discovering our rare breed chickens. Once again we were more than happy to oblige and expose our business even more and a time and date was agreed.

Unfortunately the date and the hour before the agreed time have become infamous as the day of the devastating Christchurch earthquake on February 11th 2011. We have not heard anymore from them, though that is not surprising as the the studio was based in the heart of the Red Zone in the central city which is still as I write a no go area.

I

A month or so later we were contacted by a representative of the Canterbury team of a sport that we had never heard of, Ultimate Frisbee. The art of beach and park frisbee throwing has been formalised into a team sport that is now played by millions of people around the world and much to our surprise we were about to become involved in it albeit in a very small way.

The Canterbury team was known as the Black Sheep and they must have been pretty good as they had been invited to participate in a tournament in Australia. Breaking into the big time they decided they needed to have a professional playing strip and they rang us to enquire if someone could visit us and take some photos of our black sheep.

The tournament was fast approaching and time was of the essence but unfortunately the winter weather was turning nasty and photo opportunities were not presenting themselves so in desperation they asked us if we had any photos of a black sheep we could send them. We found a lovely shot of a fully fleeced Jack the black Romney ram standing on green grass with the Red Barn in the background framed with blue sky and duly sent it off to them. Being sports lovers, especially of Canterbury teams we were more than happy to assist.

A few weeks later we received a call from the team rep once again thanking us for helping them and advising us that while not winning the tournament they had achieved a very creditable third placing, quite an achievement against the best teams in Australia. They were also sending us one of the playing strips as a thank you.

We were expecting to see a shirt featuring Jack in all his fleecy black glory accompanied by the team's name but were absolutely delighted with what emerged from the package. They had used the whole photograph and bled the blue of the sky into the rest of the strip giving it a striking light blue look and our shirt had the number 99 on its blue back.

What struck us most was the fact that the Red Barn that we use as our logo was featured nearly as prominently as Jack. Warwickz Farm was now being showcased on the playing fields of the world we told ourselves with proud smiles.

Another opportunity that we enthusiastically embraced was when we had a call from Whitebait Productions that produce a popular program for one of the television networks called Animal Academy.

The show was hosted by Sarah Ulmer, the New Zealand Olympic cycling Gold Medalist and Jeremy McGuire the head ranger at Willowbank Wildlife Reserve. We were asked if we wanted to participate in the production of an episode that would entail Warwickz Farm and our animals being featured in the six links that formed the structure of the show, leading into the programs different segments.

The first link would introduce Warwickz Farm and what we were all about and the others would feature a different type of animal. The filming would take place around the Barn, Rosie's piglet nursery and Poultry Lane.

It was an unusually cold, overcast and windy February day when the film crew of five arrived and began setting up. Sarah having a cyclist's lean body was feeling the cold and retreated to the warmth of the Barn.

I surmised that as the 'star' of the show and such a high profile sporting personality she would simply do her bits to camera and remain aloof from the rest of the proceedings in the comfort of the Barn.

"I hope you don't mind me sitting in here?" she politely asked with a rueful smile before continuing, "cos I'm bloody freezing". She turned out to be an absolute delight to work with spending much of the five hours it took to complete the filming standing outside wrapped in a blanket, laughing and joking along with everyone.

In fact both Sarah and Jeremy being animal lovers took any qualms we had about our wonderful creatures being either camera shy or just plain unhelpful away; as they patiently laughed away the many extra takes it took to get it all perfect. The first segment on our guinea pigs featured Ginny (aka Grinny) Pig and they continually fluffed their lines trying to get her intro correct, 'Grinny the Ginny guinea pig', cut!

The rabbits were probably the easiest animals to work with, sitting calmly in their arms as they introduced the different breeds. The Kunekune piglets were certainly the noisiest if not the most popular creatures with the crew as they squealed away in the firm grip of Jeremy's hands. Off camera Elaines hands were working away proffering slices of apple to keep the little fellows all in the same space.

I was just considering heading to the kitchen, during a break, to make some sandwiches and coffee for us all when a van slowly drove up the raceway to the Barn and to my delight it was the catering van dropping off a basket of delicious goodies. With the weather starting to improve the day seemed to be getting better and better. After an enjoyable half hour of showbiz feasting we were back into it.

Tracey the angora cross goat, at the time was still a young kid and full of the joys of life and was looking adorable with her long, silky white, curly locks. The idea was that Sarah would briefly interview me about her and then I would call her and she would trot into shot for a cuddle, well that was the theory anyway. After about five takes where she would run into shot uncalled for mid interview we decided it best if someone held her back. That however was not conducive to good interviewing due to the loud background noise of a very upset goatling. We ended up doing the shot with me holding her in my arms and everyone seemed very happy, especially the cameraman who was keeping a nervous eye on his supply of film.

The last link entailed a stroll with Sarah along Poultry Lane accompanied by Bartie the rooster. By now it was mid afternoon and the free rangers noticing action along the Lane and hoping for an early feed arrived in droves. It was quite an ordeal keeping straight faces as we walked along in front of the cameraman and soundman who were operating their expensive high tech equipment as they walked backwards towards the tsunami of incoming chooks, ducks, turkeys, pigeons and assorted other poultry and water fowl.

Fortunately all went well and no humans, creatures or equipment were damaged in the production that culminated in a high five from Bartie and great national publicity for Warwickz Farm.

The most regular from of exposure Warwickz Farm has, is in the alpaca show ring at the Agricultural and Pastoral (A&P) Shows we have been attending with our alpacas for over a decade now.

It sounds like an easy operation; just load your alpacas into your float and when it is time, let the judge check them out and give you your ribbons and head off home again after a look around the show. Unfortunately there is more to it then that.

The shows we usually attend are the Ellesmere and Ashburton A&P Shows and some years other ones farther afield. These shows are in October and November when the fully fleeced alpacas are looking their best and before it gets too hot for them as summer approaches.

Planning for the Shows begins early in the year when we decide which ones we are going to show, usually two three or four of them and then in August we begin the halter training for the young ones.

Bearing in mind that alpacas have only recently become domesticated, the young alpaca who has never been handled before apart from being petted, tends to take exception to being split from his paddock mates and gently restrained while a halter is placed around its' head. They all have their own personalities and some take more exception to others but they all tend to act like a bucking bronco as they take their first few steps attached to a lead rope.

We find that it takes about three weeks of consistent training of up to thirty minutes a day to get them 'show ready'. It is not only the walking that is practiced but also the standing with a model like pose while the judge pokes and prods and examines them that are polished.

Having got the young alpacas trained and the older ones back up to speed we now have the quandary of how to get them to the Show. Fortunately we have some fellow alpaca breeders who are good friends and have allowed us to use their floats over the years.

Show day arrives and we are up at sparrows fart as the alpacas need to be there and penned long before the Show opens to the public. It usually takes a bit of a push here and a pull there to get the alpacas up the ramp and into the float but once in they settle down into a sitting position on the floor and enjoy the ride.

Being curious animals our alpacas cannot believe their eyes when they see all the hustle and bustle of people and vehicles and another 100 or so other alpacas. They are always so good and calmly let us lead them to their pen where they settle in for the duration and soak up the atmosphere and the many scents that assail their flaring nostrils.

We are very proud to admit that we have never attended a Show and not come away with at least one ribbon and have a host of blue and red ribbons among our collection. What gives us the most satisfaction of all is the fact that our alpacas are competing with and matching some of the best quality alpacas in the country.

Many breeders have entered the alpaca industry fully resourced and due to the selective purchasing of bloodlines and good husbandry have herds of stunning alpacas that they regularly display at the Shows, which is what it is all about.

Our original very basic herd has over the last fifteen years due to Elaine's meticulous studies and implementation of alpaca genetics has consistently improved year by year. We have never had the funds to purchase the very best bloodlines so we have had to grow our own with the judicious use of particular stud males from a leading alpaca stud.

While much of our competitors in the show ring have the luxury of selecting from a number of alpacas for a particular class we have only one and that one is competitive and that gives us, especially Elaine, a great thrill.

Not everything goes according to plan though. A few years ago we entered a stunning honey coloured alpaca called Jolene. She had been a delight to train and we were expecting great things from her. As the judge approached her to look at her mouth and teeth, I do not know whether it was the perfume she was wearing or what it was but Jolene let go this big gob of green slime at her, pretty much at point blank range.

Alpaca judging in the show ring takes many hours and is usually a pretty sedate thing to watch but Jolene certainly livened up that mornings judging. I stood there stiffly adding my words of mortified apology to the comforting words of the stewards who I noticed were stepping out of Jolene's range. Proceedings were temporarily halted as the judge cleaned her spectacles and a steward ran off to find her a towel to wipe her unhappy green face. Suffice to say that Jolene did not end the Show with a ribbon that day.

Chapter Seventeen

Crafty Days

Elaine should really be writing this chapter as she is the craft person par excellence of Warwickz Farm while I have to have written instructions on how to thread a needle, not thank goodness that anyone has ever asked me to.

Bearing in mind my obvious biased opinion, my wife is an absolute natural when it comes to things crafty. Give her a little time and no distractions and she will very quickly master any new craft activity that appeals to her, often adding a little embellishment here or a simpler method there.

Having the blend of crafts and animals at Warwickz Farm has proved a perfect combination for our guests and visitors. Having seen all the creatures and marveled at their fleeces, fibres and furs it is fun showing our visitors what Elaine has done, and they can potentially do, with these raw materials. From carded (straightened ready for the spinning wheel) alpaca fibre to knitting yarn or the finished articles that in the Barn vary from socks, scarves, gloves and hats to waistcoats, throws, sweaters, cardigans and dresses through to fluffy dice and felted jewellery all in a range of colours and designs, often enhanced with needle felting.

In our very early days when things were even more financially stressful than they are now Elaine decided that one income stream we could kick off immediately was craft classes. A little test of the market identified that quilt making was popular and it wasn't long before Elaine had her first class booked in and ready for their patchwork quilting beginner's class.

Maybe it was booked in a little too early as Elaine in her enthusiasm to get things moving failed to remember that she was not an experienced quilter and then had to quickly find a tutor to 'assist' her in her initial classes.

Every Wednesday evening for two and a half hours the middle section of the Barn became a feverish centre of quilting activity with Elaine the most industrious 'student' soaking up all the new knowledge like a patch working sponge.

Olga, the tutor was a rather large and jovial older lady from South Africa whose close presence over the period became a little overbearing and the students, a nice mix of young mothers and sprightly grandmothers were happy to see the newly proficient Elaine take over proceedings in her own right after a few weeks.

I would provide a little light relief as I prepared the teas and coffees and biscuits mid session along with an inspection of all the works in progress, offering any humorous observations along with words of encouragement and praise. The quality of the beginners quilts to my uneducated eyes were excellent, while they all followed the same theme, for instance a row of country village shops, they were all stamped with their creators personality with the different colours and shapes built into them.

It wasn't long before someone suggested to Elaine, being a very experienced and accomplished spinner that she might like to set up a spinners group based in the Barn. The humming of spinning wheels and the sound of happy chatting became the regular theme on Wednesday evenings with the refreshments being supplied by yours truly.

Alas, as we went into the winter months with mounting bills adding up Elaine found herself having to leave the warmth of home every night to attend to her new cleaning job. The Spinners Group, now registered with Creative Fibre continued on in the Barn though without her, with it eventually getting so big it had to move to another venue.

The combination of crafts and animals has also worked very well with another income stream that we have developed and that is entertaining children during the school holidays as part of the KidsFest program and also in conjunction with primary school outings.

What is it that they say about working with children and animals? We have been lucky though over the period, with the great majority of our events being very satisfying though tiring.

Sometimes afterwards, we collapse in an exhausted heap and question whether it was all worth it for such a small financial return before remembering that over the next few months we will hopefully pick up family tours and the occasional accommodation booking and sometimes sales of rabbits, guinea pigs, piglets and so on from our efforts.

A very successful format Elaine put together for school visits involves origami, biscuit icing and a short animal tour. Dealing with large numbers of children we tend to apply the 'divide and conquer' theory and this was a perfect example of it.

The group and the teachers were divided up into three groups. The first group went on an abridged farm tour with me while one of our boys was conscripted to oversee the creative icing of the animal biscuits Elaine had baked and Elaine taught the third group how to fold little baskets into shape from the paper they had been colouring in.

When I returned with the first group the second group was waiting for me and everyone moved on to the next activity. The teachers were pleasantly surprised how smoothly and effectively the whole operation went and the children enjoyed the fact that we swore each group to secrecy about what they had been doing so as to make it a surprise for the next group. Our delighted young visitors departed Warwickz Farm with a yummy biscuit in their newly created colourful baskets and fond memories of their animal encounters.

Other children's crafty events in the Barn over the years have included classes in spinning, knitting, felting and kite making. I seriously had my doubts about the knitting and felting sessions in particular in view of modern day kids and their sophistication.

The visions I had of these kids monotonously knitting one and purling one for an hour or two was not however what Elaine had in mind. Prior to the event she knitted up some small samples of colourful basic knitting and then incorporated them into bookmarks and diary covers, cards and so on.

The youngsters using the finished articles as their inspiration eagerly learnt the basics of knitting and in quick time and with their tongues sticking out of the sides of their happy mouths created their own version of the samples to take home to impress their families.

It seems that a whole generation has been lost to traditional crafts like sewing and knitting, many of the youngsters grandmothers were good knitters but very few of their mothers so they informed us.

A month or so later Elaine and I were strolling around a shopping centre, when a young lady of about 8 years old came rushing up to us, her mother being hurriedly dragged along by her arm saying "that's the knitting lady Mum", to Elaine's delight. The novice knitter had over the weeks become a reasonably accomplished knitter according to her mother. It was a nice feeling knowing that her young life had been touched by a visit to Warwickz Farm.

Not much goes to waste on the farm and that includes wool that may not make the cut to be spun into yarn. Such wool Elaine felts, especially with the help of eager young hands who love the feel of the wet soapy wool as it gets flattened and rolled against their hands and the bamboo mats she uses.

Once the wool has been felted the real fun begins and for beginners that usually entails it being rolled and fashioned into various sized balls. Often the wool that Elaine uses for felting with young people, she has dyed a variety of bright funky colours which adds a further dimension to the whole creative experience. Balls are always a popular plaything and a bright yellow or purple ball that has a good weight and substance and has been crafted from wool from a sheep they have recently been introduced to, along with their newly learnt skill of felting makes for a memorable show and tell when the child gets home to their family.

Longer felting workshops usually involving the youngsters of families staying in the Barn include more involved but still simple procedures as the felt is manipulated into jewellery, fluffy dice and various other interesting articles.

Needle felting is a simple but very effective craft more suited to older children and adults due to the speedy manipulation of the needle which gives it that little edge. In fact that little pointy edge allowed me to add a little red dye to the process on my one and only ouchy attempt.

This technique Elaine uses to enhance garments like sweaters and hats by working various coloured felted wool into the garment and building designs into them, a current theme is bright yellow sunflowers that really bring her creation to life. She also has fun needle felting alpaca toys out of alpaca fibre and sheep toys out of wool.

Over recent years Elaine has been experimenting with different blends of fibres and wool. A mix of 80% alpaca fibre with 20% merino makes for an excellent quality knitting yarn, the extra soft and warmth of the alpaca fibre strengthened by the superfine but more resilient sheep's wool.

Many of our yarns are introduced to our visitors through the animals they have visited on the tour. For instance we currently have a quantity of some most luxurious grey wool which is a blend of Hermione a Gotland Pelt ewe with Earl our up and coming grey stud alpaca. Both animals being quite friendly would have made themselves known to our visitors as they passed by and with this knowledge our visitors look at the yarn with renewed interest and a greater understanding.

Most herds of alpacas you see around the countryside will be predominantly white; this is because they are commercial herds whose fibre is processed every year. A white fibre can be dyed any colour in a consistent shade.

We decided early on that we would go to the other extreme and breed the range of colours alpacas come in from white to brown to fawn to gray and black, with all the shades in between, a total of twelve colours. This way we would be able to showcase all the natural colours and Elaine would have the choice of these shades to mix and match with our flock of black and coloured sheep, white angora goats and white angora rabbit. Add to the mix some natural dyes, walnut, onion skin etc and the occasional splash of orange, green and purple dyes and Elaine has a wonderful palette of colour to work in to her creations.

It is fun pointing out to our visitors that the decoratively positioned ringlets of vibrant purple that they have been admiring, built into the cream felted wrap are slivers of mohair that where actually supplied by Pinot or Tracey our angora goats.

Chapter Eighteen

Mystery, Mayhem and Madness

Over the years we have experienced more strange and unusual things than we could have ever imagined at Warwickz Farm, from attending to UFOs and discovering chicken eggs with built-in buttons to having roosters sitting on eggs and discovering Elaine's horse Honey with a mysteriously plaited mane among others. It has been hard to find a chapter to cover such individual events so I have decided to put them all together here.

The first story I would like to relate is that of Basil, a mature Chinese silkie rooster who for a period, due to a shortage of available accommodation along Poultry Lane had to rough it in the pigeon loft.

One late afternoon in early spring I was doing my daily rounds of the chook houses, feeding, refreshing the water and collecting eggs and called into the pigeon loft to take care of room service for Basil.

My entry to the loft was the signal for a squadron of white fantail pigeons to push and shove their way onto the landing platform and then fight for position around the feeder.

All this sudden commotion caused Basil to shift from his comfy position in his straw strewn corner and reveal the green egg he had been sitting on.

I rubbed my eyes in amazement – a rooster in a pigeon loft is one thing, but to be sitting on an egg was another and for that egg to be green was even more astonishing.

When I say green egg I do not mean an old egg that has started to rot but an egg with a slightly green tinge to it that are laid by our aracauna chooks from South America.

After much speculation it was decided that the only logical conclusion was that I must have left a collected aracauna egg on the ground as I attended to the feeding and Basil had applied a Silkies nurturing instinct and taken responsibility for it. However the mystery deepened the following day when a second green egg appeared under him.

Now I was determined to get to the bottom of this mystery and began staking out the area. Fortunately it was not very long before I apprehended the aracauna hen who was supplying Basil with his eggs. She was located on the other side of the wall where Basil nestled in one of our aracuana coops and I caught her nudging a third egg through the gap under the wall to him. It was decided for the sanity of all concerned that Basil be relocated to a more fitting abode.

A few years ago we were given some tadpoles which we decided would be an interesting and low maintenance addition to the menagerie. We set them up in a glass tank furnished with decorously placed semi precious stones and interesting pieces of driftwood outside on a sideboard adjacent to the barbeque area.

For the top of the tank we made up a frame that could be easily lifted off and covered the top in shade cloth and then we sat back and enjoyed watching the tadpoles slowly evolve into small tree frogs.

However once fully formed three of the six frogs slowly, over the course of a week or so disappeared. You would see them as you passed by and then a few hours later one would be gone.

We searched the tank for any amphibious corpses hidden under stones or wood and looked suspiciously at the other frogs for any signs of cannibalism but the mystery remained. The top of the tank had not been dislodged and appeared secure and we were running out of answers.

We got lucky however and sprung the fourth frog making his break for freedom. The small slimy little thing had shimmied up the wall of the tank to the top and when we caught him he was squeezing through a very tight space between the tacks that held the shade cloth in place.

I would not have believed it if I hadn't have seen it. I would have thought the abrasive shade cloth would have lacerated the fine slippery skin of the frog and would have been far too painful for it to attempt, however this was obviously not the case.

Fortunately the mystery was solved while we still had some

frogs and once the shade cloth was replaced by muslin the

disappearing acts ceased.

We have had several horses over the years including Jessie,

Keybee, Honey and Fernando the miniature horse who is still

with us. This story involves Honey, Elaine's lovely chestnut

mare who originally lived in Gisborne in the North Island and

spent many years being ridden bareback by a number of children

of the greater family that owned her.

Honey settled in well and became great friends with Keybee my

large retired standardbred mare and Elaine and I enjoyed riding

together around the large 5 acre paddock which had been used as

a racehorse training track by a previous owner.

One warm spring day I decided to find the horses to brush out

some of their winter coat before the weather go too hot and was

startled to discover that honey had had a makeover. This was in the form of a neatly plaited mane. The lovely golden hair of her mane had been interlaced into sets of three knotted ropes.

Horses while being highly intelligent animals are incapable of such manual dexterity and Elaine confirmed that she had not done it. We decided that the friend of young Cody's who had stayed for a sleepover during the weekend and whose mother owned some horses must have done it.

On further investigation though that appeared not to be the case as the young man had denied doing so which also reconciled with our belief that he and Cody had spent the weekend indoors glued to the playstation.

The mystery remains to this day on who had taken the time and effort to enhance our lovely Honey. It was a one off event and I wonder if it was perhaps a horse lover whose car had broken down and had filled in the time waiting by the side of the highway talking to Honey as they went about their creative work.

Honey unfortunately was only with us for a few years before she succumbed to a heart attack. It came on very suddenly and she would not have suffered as I concluded when I found her. She had collapsed next to the fence line that she had not even had time to step away from before she keeled over and her hooves fell through the gaps in the wire netting fence as she went down.

It was a late Sunday afternoon when I noticed her laying there in the adjacent paddock as I was putting the ducks to bed. My worst fears were confirmed on closer inspection and I went to break the sad news to Elaine.

The loss of Honey was the first time we had been confronted with the death of a large animal and I wanted to dispose of the body as soon as possible, for sentimental reasons as well as health and safety ones. Our usual methods of disposal with other dead beasties had always been either burial or a funeral pyre where they were cremated however this time burial of such a large animal was not an option and the pile had recently been burnt off and so cremation was not possible either.

I rang a friend who owned several horses to seek advice and was given the phone number of a guy who I was told should be able to help. He bred and trained dogs and was always after a free source of, well, lets not go there.

I gave him a call and he told me that he would be round first thing in the morning and just as he hung up he told me that I needed to open her up to let the gases escape. I was just about to query this when I heard the burr of the dial tone.

'Open her up to let the gases escape', I repeated to myself as I sat there with a developing sinking feeling. This was during the period while I was still working full time and just dreaming of being a farmer; I clenched my soft businessman's hands in anxious anticipation and headed off to the tool shed to find a suitable knife.

I can do this; I can do this I kept telling myself as I sharpened the old carving knife, as the sparks spitting back from the newly shining blade lit up the darkening late afternoon gloom.

I don't know if I was consciously walking very slowly but the walk down the driveway and across the field seemed to take a very long time until I finally found myself squatting at the late Honeys side. I patted her still warm stomach telling her what a wonderful horse she had been and delaying the inevitable for as long as I could.

Realising the shadows were getting ever longer I positioned the knife blade along the seam in the middle of her stomach, closed my eyes and plunged it into her. I then began hacking along the seam for a couple of feet before pulling the knife out and with a shaky hand and a tearful eye examined my handiwork. Hardly what could be described as a surgical incision, but I had at least 'opened her up so that the gases could escape', I decided, before returning to the cottage where I fell into Elaine's comforting embrace.

Unfortunately there was an unpleasant part two of the operation to endure the following morning. The dog guy assumed that I would have a front end loader or some other device to lift the horse into his trailer and I had assumed that he would have a winch or something to complete the operation.

We both stood close to Honey who I was trying not to look at as her ganglia had ballooned up enormously and were now hanging out of her courtesy of my surgery, as he scratched his head in thought and I scratched mine in dismay. It hadn't helped that he was close to an hour late arriving for the pick up.

We ended up placing his trailer in a hollow in the cambered racing track close to where Honey lay and after roping her legs and attaching the length of rope to the tow bars of our old 4WD vehicles we on the second attempt were able to bounce the poor girl into the trailer as the vehicles shot over the edge of the hollow at speed. I was really not impressed with the whole episode and we have since made much better arrangements for the urgent dispatch of any large dead beasties.

I hopped out to make sure Honey was securely inside the trailer. Her body was but as the dog guy headed off with another bounce, her head hung down over the back of the trailer. I gently lifted it up back and secured it saying a fond farewell and as her head lay safely back inside, it too managed a farewell in the form of a big gob of blood that spurted out and landed on my face. It seemed to me a fitting end to a most unpleasant experience.

A more intriguing experience was the day we discovered in the aracauna chicken coop, along with two or three green tinged eggs, which by now were no longer a novelty, a couple of eggs a third of the size with a little button like protuberance, like a little nipple, at the sharp end of the egg.

We had over the years come across eggs with soft squishy shells and round eggs and also small eggs belonging to large birds but this was the first time we had found some with nipples attached. The other anomalies were usually the result of a chooks first egg being laid but what caused this aberration is still a mystery to this day.

Another mystery that was solved quite quickly, though to be totally honest not technically proven, was the discovery of a strange piece of rock I discovered as I was filling the water buckets before doing the rounds of Poultry Lane.

As you can imagine, after using the same tap day after day for years and then waiting while two 20 litre buckets of water are filled, you get to know quite intimately the space that surrounds you.

It was with some surprise therefore when I noticed a smallish piece of rock lying at my feet where no rock had lain before. Warwickz Farm has plenty of stones the majority being river stones however this was one totally different.

It was the size of a cake of soap and quite heavy with a dark grey appearance and covered in borer like holes. It was quite smooth on the edges and on one side that curved over onto itself where it had obviously broken of a larger piece.

My first thought was that it must be a part of the macadam from the highway that had broken off and been flicked off the road by a passing vehicle. I looked towards the highway that was concealed behind the ancient macrocarpa hedge and realized this couldn't have happened; besides it was too heavy a mass to be part of the road. By now the buckets were full and I dropped it back on the ground and continued my chores.

Later that evening I found myself still mystified by this enigmatic piece of rock and by a process of elimination decided that the only direction it could have come from was above. I decided to google space rock images and within seconds I was staring at a variety of shapes and sizes of the piece of rock I had chucked back on the ground a few hours earlier.

The borer like holes were caused by atmospheric pressure and the smoothness would have been caused when it became super heated and then later cooled down. First thing the next morning, after checking that my hands didn't have a radioactive green glow to them, I retrieved my now identified flying object and found a nice play to display it in the Barn.

So far we have not had it tested but I am almost certain that it has come from the skies above and besides why risk debunking a great story. I am very pleased though that I was not standing there waiting for the buckets to fill with water when it did arrive

or I may not now be here to share this story with you.

Epilogue

While this book has been the story of how Elaine and I along with our wonderful animals created a unique lifestyle and business I couldn't finish without acknowledging and thanking the wonderful two legged creatures who have been part of our journey.

Bruce Warwick, Elaine's ex husband works as a boat builder and likes nothing better, like most people, than to come home and have a glass of wine and curl up in front of the television. Over the years he was nodded cynically to himself as he overhears our plans for the farm, thinking to himself 'oh yeah we will see', and over the years he has seen.

To give him his due though, he does get off the couch and helps out particularly when we have been busy with guests. Having a handy, handyman around has also been very helpful over the years. You will notice the large number and variety of chicken coops along Poultry Lane; well the rustic looking ones are mine, while the more conventional ones are Bruce's. He is also a far better trailer backer upper than I will ever be.

The boys, Dean, Adam and Cody while being devoted aficionados of high tech entertainment of the various sized screen technology have also been available when required to help out with guests and animals over the years.

They have also been very understanding when the financial resources have not been available to do for them what we may otherwise have been able to if we hadn't pursued our dream.

The same goes for my three children in Sydney, Joshua, Stewart and Madelyn, who have shared the journey from a distance with the occasional memorable visit.

Brenda and Neil Lester, fellow alpaca breeders who have become good friends over the years have very generously lent us their alpaca float for many of the Shows we have attended. They have been very supportive of our venture and Brenda, a fellow crafter was instrumental with Elaine in getting the Selwyn Spinners Group off the ground.

As they say 'a friend in need is a friend indeed' and Neil and Brenda have many times offered us sanctuary in times of floods, snow blizzards and so on, fortunately none of which so far, have we had to accept.

Rose Gilbert, a very long time friend of Elaine's has also donated her float to the cause over the years. Another alpaca breeder, she has worked closely with us in improving the grey genetics of our herd.

Nic Cooper and Linda Blake from Southern Alpacas have been working with us and our alpacas for 15 years now and have been instrumental slowly but surely in the creation of our top quality herd of nice natured alpacas.

Every farm needs the services of a good vet and a rare breed's farm needs the services of a rare breed of vet and that's who we have in Monique Koning. Trained as a medical doctor in her native Holland Monique retrained as a vet in New Zealand. What could be better than having a vet with a bedside manner?

Monique is a mobile vet which is perfect for our requirements and she has become a friend too over the years, always mindful of our financial situation.

Long time friends of Elaine's are Patricia and Colin Winder. Now getting on in age they have been very supportive of Warwickz Farm over the years. They help us keep our ever growing compost heap under control by utilizing sackfuls of it in their lovely country garden.

Pat's huge enthusiasm for life and cheerful disposition and sense of mischief never fail to give us a boost when times are hard.

There are a host of others who have helped us over the period with our rare breeds and supplies and crafts including Sitereh and Rowena with our rabbits, Gavin with our poultry, Carmel with our guinea pigs, Barry with our hay, Nic with our home kill and Bev with our crafts.

A special mention goes to Boon, a captain with Singapore Airlines who stayed with us a few years ago with his family and has remained in touch often bringing flight crew for visits and talking us up across the world.

Another special mention goes to Chantal Stallard the bravest girl we know, daughter of my oldest friend Tony. Chantal aged 12 is battling leukemia and I have been sharing life on the Farm with her in a weekly letter. She has made us appreciate how precious life is and how lucky we are to live one such as ours.

I would finally like to thank you dear reader for giving us the opportunity to relive our journey and share it with you, I hope you have enjoyed it as much as we have so far.

8990302R00147

Printed in Great Britain
by Amazon.co.uk, Ltd.,
Marston Gate.